THE DAY TRADER'S COURSE

Outperform the Dow / Gunter Meissner and Randall Folsom

Pattern, Price & Time / James A. Hyerczyk

Point and Figure Charting, Second Edition / Thomas J. Dorsey

Schwager on Futures / Jack Schwager

Seasonality / Jake Bernstein

Stock Index Futures & Options / Susan Abbott Gidel

Stock Market Course / George A. Fontanills and Tom Gentile

Stock Market Course Workbook / George A. Fontanills and Tom Gentile

Study Guide for Trading for a Living / Dr. Alexander Elder

Study Guide to Accompany Fundamental Analysis / Jack Schwager

Study Guide to Accompany Technical Analysis / Jack Schwager

Technical Analysis / Jack Schwager

Technical Analysis of the Options Markets / Richard Hexton

Technical Market Indicators / Richard J. Bauer Jr. and Julie R. Dahlquist

Trader Vic II / Victor Sperandeo

Trader's Tax Solution / Ted Tesser

Trading Applications of Japanese Candlesticks Charting / Gary Wagner and
    Brad Matheny

Trading Chaos / Bill Williams

Trading for a Living / Dr. Alexander Elder

Trading Game / Ryan Jones

Trading in the Zone / Ari Kiev, M.D.

Trading Systems & Methods, Third Edition / Perry Kaufman

Trading the Plan / Robert Deel

Trading to Win / Ari Kiev, M.D.

Trading with Crowd Psychology / Carl Gyllenram

Trading with Oscillators / Mark Etzkorn

Trading without Fear / Richard W. Arms, Jr.

Ultimate Trading Guide / John Hill, George Pruitt, and Lundy Hill

Value Investing in Commodity Futures / Hal Masover

Visual Investor / John J. Murphy

THE DAY TRADER'S COURSE

*Low-Risk, High Profit Strategies
for Trading Stocks and Futures*

Lewis Borsellino
with
Patricia Crisafulli

JOHN WILEY & SONS, INC.
New York • Chichester • Weinheim • Brisbane • Singapore • Toronto

Published by John Wiley & Sons, Inc.
Published simultaneously in Canada.

This publication is designed to provide accurate and authoritative information in regard to the subject matter covered. It is sold with the understanding that the publisher is not engaged in rendering professional services. If professional advice or other expert assistance is required, the services of a competent professional person should be sought.

Designations used by companies to distinguish their products are often claimed by trademarks. In all instances where the author or publisher is aware of a claim, the product names appear in Initial Capital letters. Readers, however, should contact the appropriate companies for more complete information regarding trademarks and registration.

Library of Congress Cataloging in Publication Data:

Borsellino, Lewis J., 1957–
    The day trader's course / Lewis Borsellino with Patricia Crisafulli.
      p. cm.—(Wiley trading)
    Includes index.
    ISBN 0-471-06515-3
    1. Day trading (Securities) 2. Electronic trading of securities. I. Crisafulli, Patricia. II. Title. III. Series.
HG4515.95 .B673   2001
332.64'2'0285—dc21   2001045304

10 9 8 7 6 5 4 3 2 1

For my wife, Julie, and my children:
Joey, Briana, Anthony, Lewis, Nick, Jamie, and Nicole

Acknowledgments

Trading is a solitary endeavor. Whether you trade at home, in a trading room, or on the floor of an exchange, it's you versus the market.

But as a profession, trading is really a community. In this book, I wish to salute all the traders, brokers, and clerks who ever put on a jacket at the Chicago Merc and at our sister exchanges across the country. I welcome into our profession the new breed of screen traders, who will help to revolutionize this business.

I also want to thank the entire team at TeachTrade.com, specifically: my partner, Brad Sullivan; our technician, Jim Sebanc; Vince Allegra; Pat Tabet; and my cousin and friend, Bob Borsellino, as well as Brenda Hilfiker of DTN and our graphic artist Mark Smith.

And finally, I acknowledge my coauthor and TeachTrade.com site editor, Tricia Crisafulli. Without her talent, experience, and dedication, this book could not have been written.

L.B.

Preface

Trading is a profession unlike any other. It requires a unique set of skills and requires discipline all its own. No matter what your background, personal or professional, when you begin trading you must start at step one.

My goal in writing this book is to give you an introduction into the discipline and techniques of trading. The lessons include the topics I feel are the most important for any trader, in any market: mental preparation, technical analysis, devising a trading plan, trade execution, and, above all, discipline.

When I started trading some 20 years ago, I learned by working with and watching some of the best traders in the business. It was a different world then at the Chicago Mercantile Exchange, a place I'm proud to have called my professional home for two decades. Trading was done in the pit exclusively. The term "electronic trading" was not part of our vocabulary.

Today, the computer screen has brought the market to traders like you, wherever you are. This has made for profound changes in how futures and stocks trade, and will trade in the future. But there are timeless lessons that are as valid today as they were 20 years ago and undoubtedly will be 20 years hence.

This book contains those lessons, especially of the psychological and emotional variety, as well as the techniques we use to trade in some of the most active and volatile markets in the world—namely the Standard & Poor's (S&P) 500 and Nasdaq futures.

Trading is best learned by doing, especially with a mentor or guide to help you. While I can't sit at your side (obviously) as you trade, I wanted to replicate the kind of teaching and coaching that we give the traders we bring on board at our company, TeachTrade.com. Seeing what we see in a chart, understanding our interpretation of the market, and dissecting our trade executions, I believe, will give you the best insight into what trading is all about.

As you trade, you will also learn lessons about yourself, particularly how well you master your emotions, your ego, and your ability to take losses and to keep profits in perspective.

Good luck . . . and good trading.

Contents

1

The Mental Game

At first you thought it was going to be easy. You read the hype and hoopla that day trading would bring you the sun, moon, and stars. You opened an online account and jumped into trading with both feet. You scored on the first few trades. It seemed too easy to be true: You bought a stock. It went up. You sold at a profit. What you didn't realize, however, was that in 1999 the market as a whole was up. As the old saying goes, "A rising tide raises all boats." In this case, the market's upward surge brought the majority of stocks with it.

Then came the downturn. The Nasdaq Composite, the highflier that had posted nearly an 86 percent gain in 1999, ended 2000 with a loss of more than 39 percent. The Standard & Poor's 500-stock cash index (S&Ps), the benchmark for individual stock and fund performance, declined 10 percent from the close of 1999 to the close of 2000.

Even on the last trading day of the year—December 29, 2000—the Nasdaq Composite index dropped 63 points or 2.5 percent to 2493. Cisco Systems Inc. (CSCO) and Microsoft Corporation (MSFT) led the way downward, with Cisco trading off $1^3/_8$ at $38^3/_{16}$ and Microsoft down $1^5/_{16}$ at $43^1/_4$. ("U.S. Tech Stocks Fall on Final Trading Day of Year 2000," Reuters, December 29, 2000.)

Blame the "tech wreck," or recession fears, or overzealous activity efforts by the Federal Reserve in 1999 to curb a runaway economy. Whatever the reason, the market was down. Period.

As all traders know, you can't ignore the facts. The price on the screen is as immutable as the fingerprints on your own hands. You can't change the price by an act of will any more than you can make time stand still. And the fact was (and is) the much-touted new millennium raised far more questions about the new economy than Wall Street had answers. The suffix ".com" no longer was a license to print money (or raise it from eager venture capitalists). "Flight to quality" meant out of Nasdaq and its dominant tech sector and into household names. Even a surprise rate cut early in 2001 by the Federal Reserve wasn't enough to jump-start the markets and keep them running positively.

As we write in first quarter 2001, the talk is of economic slowdown and the possibility of recession, with all eyes on Mr. Greenspan & Co. to bail us out. Markets and leading stocks continue to struggle. Traders who had ridden on the bulls' coattails are now nose-to-nose with the bear.

In the trading arena, a bear market is what separates the amateurs from the pros. Put another way, welcome to the trader's law of physics: What goes up must come down—often in gyrations and sometimes with ever-increasing volatility and for reasons that may confound you. The result can be panic and confusion. Fearful of losing money, the uninitiated cling to positions that move increasingly into the red—until they face a margin call on a deflated stock or the brokerage house yanks them out of a futures position.

Clearly, they have neglected the cardinal rule of trading: **Always protect against losses. Profits take care of themselves.**

In this book I will address not only the how-to's of technical analysis and trade execution, but, more important, the mental discipline that must be a part of every trade. You can never underestimate the mental side of trading, whether you're placing your first order through a broker or you've been trading successfully for years. Discipline is as much a part of my trading plan today as it was when I first walked onto the floor of the Chicago Mercantile Exchange 20 years ago.

It was a different world then. In 1981, stock index futures had not been launched as yet at the Chicago Mercantile Exchange, where I still trade today. I started out as a 22-year-old runner and clerk at the "Merc," an apprentice to Maury Kravitz, a major trader in those days at the exchange. After a few months, I became a broker, filling customer orders in the gold futures pit, a contract that is no longer traded in Chicago. Later, I traded for my own account and filled orders, since dual-trading was allowed at the Merc in those days.

It was a tough learning curve for me just as it was—and is—for every beginning trader. Your expectation is that you'll make money at this, because you want to make money. But don't be discouraged if you don't see any profit the first year. In fact, if you can just cover your cost of trading the first year, you should consider yourself a success. The most important lesson for you, particularly in the first year, is to learn how to take losses—quickly, with a clear head, and without panic. In my first year of trading, I was barely able to cover my costs. I had to take a job at night to support myself. I nearly gave up, I was so discouraged.

What I couldn't see then was that I was gaining a valuable education in the University of the Market that would serve me well over the years. Then, when a lucky out-trade (see Glossary) netted me a windfall of $57,000, I had ample capital for the first time. I headed to the hot new pit at the Merc—the S&P futures pit—and I never left. But I went to that market a wiser trader. I had withstood the test of the market. I had endured losses and kept my head when I made profit.

Today, I trade in the S&P pit on the floor of the Merc for an hour or two a day. Then, I trade or monitor my position at the screen at my Chicago-based trading firm, where I also run an educational and market commentary web site for traders, TeachTrade.com.

I've gone through a lot of change as a trader. But one thing that remains constant is the psychological side of trading. Trading is a mental game. The emotional and psychological aspects of trading can never be overlooked or underestimated. For one thing, there is the motivation of trading. (*Yeah*, you say to yourself, *it's money, right?*) Well, if it were only the money, then most of us would have found something else to do. If you doubt that, consider the failure rate of traders. In equities, those who try day trading last about six months. In futures, the average life span is about three months, although trading activity dwindles significantly in the latter two months.

The one thing I know about trading is that it's infectious. Once you've made a couple of trades and turned a profit, it gets into your blood. The most successful traders I've known live and breathe trading and the markets. The money is part of it, to be sure. But a bigger part is the adrenaline rush you get from the market. You can also tell this from the retail side of the trading business with average investors and speculators who trade through a broker. Many times beginning traders who try their hand at this will lose their capital, but they don't close their accounts. They leave a small amount to keep them open, and as soon as they get some more capital to trade, they try again.

Now, before you tell yourself that this won't happen to you, that you'll somehow beat the odds, remember that the success rate among traders is slim. The only way to improve your chances of survival— and there is no guarantee—is with education. That is the purpose of *The Day Trader's Course.*

Whether you trade stocks, futures, or even options, you must have a carefully executed plan. You shouldn't buy because you heard a tip at the health club or on television. Your trades ought to be the result of the execution of your plan. And if your trade goes against you, the next step is a reexamination of that plan to learn what went wrong and what you'll do differently next time.

The foundation of this plan is technical analysis, which will be addressed at length in later chapters. But the quality that must be developed and maintained—first, last, and always—is discipline. More than an analytical mind and the ability to make quick decisions, discipline is an attribute that will keep you in the trading game. Discipline allows you to make the best decisions based on the market conditions (not your ego, your need to make money, or your fear of loss). And discipline will allow you to execute your trades according to plan, including getting stopped out of a trade.

There are highs and lows in trading equivalent to those experienced in a competitive sporting event. When you're trading, it's the ultimate David versus Goliath situation, for it is truly you versus the market. Whether you're a one-lot trader or an institution swinging around

1,000-contract positions, you are still in competition with the market-place at large. When you place that trade, you are putting everything on the line—not only the money involved in that trade, but your research and analysis, your decision-making process, and your execution. You will face the ego challenge of knowing that, at least some of the time, you will be wrong.

Each time you trade, you are weighing the success and/or failure of your plan. And if you do have a profitable trade, the challenge then becomes even harder: You must not allow your ego to be clouded by your financial success so that you can't keep a clear sight on your plan. What you savor is not the money that you've made, but rather the fact that you've successfully executed your plan. If you don't think this kind of successful challenge is the primary motivating factor, ask anyone who has launched or built a business. Entrepreneurs will tell you that the payoff was not the money they made, but the fact that they were successful in conceiving, developing, and merchandising an idea. And, as in trading, it all started with a plan.

The first step in drafting that plan begins long before the market opens and you sit down to trade. It begins with your psychological preparedness. You couldn't launch yourself into trading without this kind of conditioning any more than you'd set out for a cross-country run without stretching exercises. When I discuss trading, I use a lot of sports analogies because of the parallels of intensity, physical and mental demands, ego control, risks, and rewards. For traders, this preparation is a daily routine that will be a personal ritual.

For me, that means an hour workout in my home gym or, when the weather is fair, an hour at the golf course chipping balls onto the green. Your choice of preparation may be jogging, meditation, yoga, tai-chi, or whatever. But there must be an activity—I prefer a physical one—that tells your mind, "Okay, it's time to get ready for trading. The rest of my life has to be put aside for now."

You can't trade effectively during times of personal problems, disruptions, or distractions. If something is weighing on your mind—whether it's an illness in the family or even a positive event such as buying a new house or the birth of a child—it can and will affect your trading. If you can't sufficiently clear your mind, you won't be able to apply unwavering concentration to your trading. Better just to do your homework for that day, watching the market, studying the charts and indicators, than to put your money on the line. If you decide to trade, reduce your trade size so that you have less at risk. Don't bemoan the big money you could have made; be glad you had the discipline to limit your exposure.

The backbone of mental discipline is to focus on the trade, not the money. This isn't easy for the novice or even the professional trader. In fact, professional traders face a special breed of mental demon, born of their own successes. I've wrestled with these demons on more than one occasion.

The problem comes when you know you can make money, and a good deal of it, by trading. You've had five-figure and six-figure days. So when the money pressure is on, you think you can work your magic in the market. Your focus shifts from making a good trade to making good money. The result is almost always disaster. As we'll discuss in Chapter 5, you have to trade what the market gives you, which will play a large role in your profit potential on any given day.

What occurs is usually something like this: You go into the market saying, "I'm going to make a lot of money today." Or maybe you say, "I *need* to make a lot of money today," either to make up for previous losses, to put a down payment on a bigger house, or to buy that boat/car/vacation property/whatever that you've always wanted.

Complicating this factor is that you know you've had big days in the past. But, if you examine them, those big days were the result of market opportunities that you reaped for large profits. Put another way, you successfully executed a plan that, coupled with market conditions that you analyzed properly, yielded a profit.

But if those market conditions do not exist—if the market is thin in terms of volume or participation, rangebound, or quiet—then you may be forcing trades that won't materialize. You'll trade too big or too frequently and risk too much. Instead of big profits, you may end up with the exact opposite.

Your goal is to develop a positive mental attitude and to have confidence in your ability to make good trades and to move quickly beyond the losing trades.

Legends, Language, and Lore of Traders

As you trade, you will face your own personal demons. There is greed and its best friend, fear. And of course there is ego. Now, to trade you have to have a sense of confidence and the ability to make a decision, which may be the by-product of a good, healthy ego. But beware of letting your ego become so big that it clouds your judgment and skews your decision making.

Here's a case in point: In the early part of 1987, at the age of 30, I made $4.5 million trading my own money. I was trading with such size that all the order fillers came to me. I was used to trading big, and everybody in the pit knew it—and my ego liked that. The problem was, after the crash of October 1987, liquidity dried up considerably. As a result, I was trading too big for the market. In the end, I made about $100,000—before expenses—trading, and I had huge swings in profitability that year.

That's when I learned a valuable lesson about trading what the market gives you. I couldn't fling around hundreds of contracts just to satisfy my ego or because people in the pit expected that of me. I had to trade what suited both my own plan and the market conditions. After that, my trading was noticeably back on track.

In my career, I've seen so many talented young traders blow it because they lacked the discipline or the ability to take on risk. Either they took on too much risk and lost all their capital in one or a few trades, or they became the proverbial deer in the headlights when it came to risk. The underlying factor was they failed at the mental game of trading. The singular problem was a focus on the money and not on the trade. But admittedly, it's a tough lesson to become unemotional about money.

In my own experience there have been times when I've been up $17,000 and I'd like to make $3,000 more—just to have a nice round profit number of $20,000. So, I keep trading for the extra $3,000—even though the market may have quieted down and there are no longer that many opportunities to trade. When I'm on the floor, that absence of volume is palpable. When the market is busy, the S&P pit is packed with people—about 500 of them—all shouting, screaming, waving their arms, and gesturing wildly with their hands. When it's quiet, the noise level and activity are far less. And when it's dead . . . well, I've seen times when traders have tossed a nerf football around the pit they're so bored.

When the market conditions don't warrant—on their own—an objective reason to trade, it's better to quit for the day. Sticking around just to make some more money is not a good motivation. There have been times when, trying to make another $3,000, I lose the $17,000 I had in the first place.

Then there are the days when I'm down, say, $15,000. I'll stay in the pit to make it back, even though I know I should cut my losses, take a break, and regroup. The temptation, even after all these years, is to stay in the pit and keep trading to make it back—even though the market conditions aren't there. The problem is that by focusing on the money and losing sight of the trading conditions I am at a higher risk for further loss. What I'm trying to tell you candidly is that even after 20 years and much success, I still fight these demons. In fact, it's a bigger mistake for an experienced trader to think that he or she won't face them.

The best days happen when a trader is prepared and the market presents opportunities that can be capitalized upon. The more volatility, the more opportunity to make money. Day traders and short-term traders live on volatility. But when ranges are tight, volume is light, and the market is slow, it's not worth the time—or the risk—to trade. The opportunity just isn't there.

One of the signs of experience for a trader is to know when to trade . . . and when to wait. Overtrading, chasing the market, risk and reward out of balance—all of which we'll discuss in later chapters— are pitfalls that await every trader, no matter how experienced. There are simply days—and times—when it's best to sit on the sidelines. You study the market on days like that, keeping your mind in—but your money out. For example, you may find it's better to be on the sidelines the day before a Federal Reserve meeting—and the market is anticipating some kind of interest-rate action—and the morning of the day the Fed will make its announcement.

It may not be easy to make yourself sit on the sidelines. If you have a regular day job—with a salary, benefits, and the security that you'll be paid on Friday—it's not so difficult to take a day off. If you're sick or you take a personal day, you may be a little busier when you go back, going through the voice mail and sifting through the e-mail, or maybe putting in another hour or so to make a deadline. But you'll still get paid. When you don't trade, however, you don't have the chance to make money. For beginning traders, the temptation is to be in the market all the time. The more they trade, they tell themselves, the more money they'll make. But, as I outlined earlier, you must be in the market at the most opportune times. Because if the timing is wrong or your mental discipline isn't there, then you're faced with the possibility that the more you trade, the more you'll lose.

That's a harder lesson to grasp than you might think. For one thing, the lure of making money—big money—is very strong in trading. And those who are new to the game usually have the fever; they want to trade. I remember when I was starting out, and over the years I've trained many young traders in the pit. More recently, we've brought some aspiring young screen-traders into B&S Trading (for Borsellino and Sullivan), the day-to-day operation of which is overseen by my partner, Brad Sullivan, one of the most talented traders I've ever had the privilege to work with.

Over the years, I've met countless wanna-be traders. Too many of them end up being a casualty statistic because they underestimate what they're up against. It doesn't matter what your professional background is—you could be a doctor, a lawyer, a nuclear scientist— trading is an entirely different endeavor that requires a unique set of disciplines, techniques, and strategies that must be learned and employed to trade.

Here's an analogy that may prove to be helpful. When I learned to play golf, I was told that this was a "game of misses." No one—not even a pro—hits a perfect shot every time. But the difference between pros and the rest of us is that the pros' misses are slight compared with ours. In other words, they don't miss by as much. Trading is the same thing. No one trades perfectly. No one can pick the top and the bottom every time, or identify every move. But the professional traders, thanks to their experience, have fewer "market misses" than the novices. They know how to cut their losses, regroup for the next trade, and execute—without damaging their confidence and second-guessing their abilities in the process.

The other thing that many traders don't fully comprehend is that they are entering a competitive arena dominated by experienced traders, professionals, and institutions. It's like being a fish in a shark tank.

When you start trading, you will have losses. In fact, with the traders that I've sponsored and trained over the years, I never expected them to turn a profit the first year. The best outcome to anticipate for the first year is to cover expenses. We give a similar message on our web site, TeachTrade.com, telling traders not to expect to do more than cover expenses the first year. Expectations higher than this are an invitation to a fall.

Many people who go into trading have an entirely different perspective. They want to make money—lots of it. And they expect to make it tomorrow. Ironically, it's this kind of attitude that undercuts a trader's potential to make money. They're so focused on making money that they can't trade effectively.

Here are some examples that are representative of a lot of wannabes out there.

"Joe" is in the building trades, an occupation he now sees as limiting. He believes he can do more with his life and his intelligence in a different field. He wants to try his hand at full-time trading. He's been dabbling part-time, and he's managed to turn a modest profit. He has $5,000 to start trading, and he's ready to go into this full-time. The only problem for Joe is that once he quits his current day job, he won't have another source of income. He has a wife, who doesn't work outside the home, two small children, and a $1,500 monthly mortgage.

"Jane" is a 22-year-old with the "trading bug." She spent six months working as a clerk for minimum wages to learn the ropes of the market. Her family has given her $20,000 to start trading. But instead of keeping her monthly living expenses to a minimum, Jane rents an apartment in downtown Chicago. Her expenses of rent, food, and entertainment are $3,000 a month.

Both Joe and Jane are starting out with tremendous disadvantages by underestimating the learning curve. Their lifestyles and their lack of outside financial cushions demand that they make money their first year of trading. That means, from day one, they are going to focus on the money—and not on making trades. To start out with the premise that you *must* make money is potentially deadly.

To be a trader, you must take a different view of money—or more specifically the money in your account. It's not a profit, and it's not money to be spent. Rather, it's "raw material inventory." You can't trade without this inventory money any more than a paper mill could operate without pulp. If you deplete your inventory to pay your bills and finance your lifestyle, you will seriously hamper your potential as a trader. Moreover, you've increased the probability of becoming a casualty statistic.

Now let's take the case of "Bill," who has been trading on the side for three years. The first year, he gave back as much as he made trading. The second year he did a little better, and the third year he made a good profit. He has $25,000 to trade and a $15,000 nest egg that he vows he won't touch. Further, his wife works outside the home and has an ample salary to meet the family's financial obligations. Bill has reached the point in his life and in his career that he has to make a change. His trading is getting in the way of his day job. With his wife's blessing, Bill is going to quit his job and trade full-time.

Obviously, Bill is starting out against a far different backdrop than are Joe and Jane. He can scratch the first year—meaning no profit and no significant loss after expenses—and still do okay. Without that pressure to make money, Bill has the best likelihood actually to make money, at least compared to Joe and Jane. Put another way, think of the old saying, "Desperate people do desperate things." In trader's lingo, "Desperate traders take on too much risk and almost certainly blow up."

Legends, Language, and Lore of Traders

Most traders have an innate respect for money. It's our raw material with which we make our living. And, of course, it's what pays our mortgages, feeds our families, and sends our kids to college.

When I have a bad day, I have a ritual that reminds me about the value of money. If I lose a few thousand, I go out and buy something—a new suit for myself, something my wife has had her eye on, or something for the kids. Then I look at that item (or items) I have just purchased. I tally up what I've spent. That brings home, in a tangible way, what money is. When you trade, sometimes you can become disassociated with the value of money. You're trying not to focus on the money, so it may seem like playing with poker chips. But while you don't focus on money, you can't lose respect for it.

I remember one of my early lessons about respect for money, taught to me by my mentor, Maury Kravitz. I was in my mid-20s and I had just had a big day—a six-figure day. Maury and I were out to breakfast.

When the check came, I grabbed it before Maury could. The total was $6. I gave the waitress $20 and told her, "Keep the change."

"Why did you do that?" Maury asked me.

"I had a big day. She works hard. So I figured I'd give her a big tip," I replied.

"Then why didn't you leave her $100? That would have really made her day," Maury said.

I was beginning to see his point. With a $6 bill, a 20 percent tip would have been $1.20! The $14 tip I gave the waitress was generous, but I was in danger of thinking that the money didn't mean anything.

"Just because you had a big day," Maury told me, "doesn't mean you can lose respect for money. Because when you're trading, you can lose money just as fast as you got it."

Remember: the market, not the money. Think about making good trades, not about making money. Focus on the trading process. If that process is sound, the outcome will be a profit.

What goes on in your mind is a vital part of how you trade. For that reason, let's review what I call my Ten Commandments of Trading. If you follow them more often than not, you'll keep yourself on the path to trader heaven (which is, of course, buying low and selling high). Trader hell is when everything starts out so promising—and then it all blows up.

Commandment 1. Trade for success, not for money. Your motivation is the well-executed trade. We all want to do well and reap the financial rewards. But the goal is success itself. In the case of trading, this is the feeling of accomplishment that comes from a well-executed trade, based on technical research.

Commandment 2. Be disciplined. As I stated previously, the one quality that traders must possess above all others is discipline. The ability to master your mind, your body, and your emotions is the key to trading. You can have the best technical analysis available, but without discipline, it will be difficult—if not impossible—to execute trades consistently and profitably. Remember this: The disciplined trader—regardless of profit or loss—comes back to trade another day.

Commandment 3. Know yourself. Are you the kind of person who can handle risk, or do you break out in a cold sweat at the mere thought of risking something—such as your own capital? If the thought of putting money on the line makes you unable to sleep at night, then a diversified, low-risk stock and fixed income stock portfolio may be all you can handle when it comes to participation in the financial markets. But if you can handle risk in a disciplined fashion, then perhaps trading is for you. Remember, the key here is handling risk with discipline. Over the years, I've talked with countless people who think they would be naturals at trading because they love going to Las Vegas, and they can "really lay it on the line" when they're at the gaming table. If you want to gamble—go to Vegas. If you want to use discretionary capital to make well-executed trades based on technical analysis, then consider trading.

Commandment 4. *Lose your ego.* The quickest way to end your career as a trader is to let your ego influence your decision making. And the more successful you are as a trader, the bigger the challenge this will be. You need to silence your ego in order to listen to the market, to follow what your technical analysis is indicating and not what you think *should* happen. When you can put yourself aside and bow to the whims of the market, then you will have a greater chance of success. But believing that you are successful because you possess a certain skill—or, more dangerously, to believe that you have mastered the market—is a path to almost certain ruin. At the same time, you cannot be so emotionally fragile that unprofitable trades shatter your confidence. When you trade, put your ego aside. Allow yourself to get out of losing positions quickly, even if that means the humbling experience of having the market prove you wrong. And when you're successful, never let it go to your head. This is often difficult for people who have been high achievers. They have to realize that part of the trading plan is dealing with a loss.

Commandment 5. *Understand that there's no such thing as hoping, wishing, or praying when it comes to the market.* The market goes up when there are more buyers than sellers, and it goes down when the opposite occurs. It doesn't, however, rise because you will it to do so, nor does it fall because you're short and you pray that it will go down. I've seen too many traders, staring panic-stricken at the computer screen, actually beg the market to move one way or another. The reason? They're stuck in a losing position and won't get out because they hope, wish, and pray that the market will turn around and go their way. The reality is on the screen. When the market hits your stop-loss level (the predetermined price at which you'll cut your losses), get out. Even if the market then turns around and rallies in your face, you should congratulate yourself for having discipline. If you have solid money-managment skills, you can have a loss and still keep trading.

Commandment 6. *Let your profits run and cut your losses quickly.* This goes with Commandment 5. Know your risk level, and, when you hit your stop-loss point, exit the trade. As we'll discuss in later chapters on execution, always trade with stops. When you have a small loss, get out. Then reevaluate the market and execute a new trade. At the same time, know how to let your profits run, but don't be greedy. If you trade using technical analysis, you'll determine your entry and exit points before you place the trade. Then when the signals are confirmed, you make the trade. When you hit the profit target, get out. You'll never go broke taking a profit. Don't get greedy and hang onto a profitable trade so long that the market turns against you suddenly and then you have a loser.

Commandment 7. Know when to trade and when to wait. As we discussed earlier, it is not practical or possible to trade every day, all day. You trade when your analysis, your system, and your strategy say that you have a buy or sell to execute. If the market doesn't have a clear direction, then wait on the sidelines until it does. Meanwhile, keep your mind on the market, but keep your money out of it.

Commandment 8. Love your losers like you love your winners. Maybe even more. Losing trades will be your best teachers. When you have a losing trade, it's because of some flaw in your analysis or your judgment. Or perhaps the market simply didn't do what you thought it would. Maybe you're trying to trade breakouts, and the market is rangebound. Or perhaps you were chasing the market, jumping on the uptrend too late when the market had already topped out. When you have a losing trade, something is out of sync with the market. Determine what went wrong—objectively; then adjust your thinking, if necessary, and enter the trade again.

Commandment 9. After three losing trades in a row, take a break. If you've just had three losing trades this is not the time to take on more risk, but rather to become extremely disciplined. Sit on the sidelines for a while. Watch the market. Clear your head. Reevaluate your strategy, and then put on another trade.

Consider the story of an S&P trader we profiled on TeachTrade.com who trades out of his home in the Smoky Mountains. On October 12, 1999, the trader recalls, he went long at the opening bell, only to have the market go against him—and keep going against him "until that uncle point was reached yet again, three losers in a row." The losses reached the point, the trader says, that he still doesn't want his wife to know! He took a break, drove to a quiet place, and thought about things—his life, his trading. Then he went back to trade the afternoon session, starting small and building back his confidence.

"By the end of the day, I had gotten it all back, and had a few dollars to the plus side," the trader recalls. "That day taught me that all the indicators, systems, books, videos, web sites, and advisers mean nothing unless you, yourself, are willing to apply them—and apply them on every trade, to every setup, to every entry, to every stop placement, and to every exit."

Commandment 10. Observe the unbreakable rule. As we all know, you can break a rule and get away with it once in a while. But one of these days, the rules will break you. *If you continually violate these Ten Commandments of Trading, you will eventually pay for it with your profits.* That's the unbreakable rule. If you have trouble with any of these Commandments, come back and read this one. Then read it again.

The goal of these Commandments is to help you keep your head in the game while your money is on the line. Just as the professional athlete—from the golfer to the football player—has rituals and exercises to prepare mentally and physically for the next game, so must traders condition themselves before the bell rings. Certainly, when I began trading there was the physical demand of standing—sometimes from bell to bell—in the trading pit, arms extended over my head until I thought my hands had turned into 100-pound weights. Physical fatigue is a big factor for many floor traders (and why the 40-something veterans like me are gladly trading upstairs at the screens).

But even at the screen, you need full concentration when you're in the market. For someone who has always been physically active— whether it was high school and college football or a workout at the gym today—I believe exercising my body keeps my mind sharp. That's why the first step in preparing to trade is to clear your mind of distractions. If your money is in the market, your brain had better be there, too. You can't be thinking, worrying, daydreaming, or obsessing about anything else.

Next, have realistic expectations about your physical and mental limitations. Yes, when I was a young trader I stood in the pit from bell to bell, largely because I was filling orders for customers. But it is not realistic for *any* trader to expect to sit in front of a computer from 8 A.M. Central time (a half hour before the market opens) until 4 P.M. (45 minutes after equity index futures close) five days a week. You must take a break. Work smart. Concentrate your trading time during the first 90 to 120 minutes of trading, and then take a break. Regroup your thoughts. Do some more research, and then prepare anew for the final 90 to 120 minutes of trading.

Even when I was in the pit for the entire session in my early days, I saw that the best opportunities (and frankly the busiest times for customer orders) were from the open at 8:30 A.M. Central time until 10 A.M., and then again around 1:30 P.M. until the close. The rest of the time, I usually got chopped up in thin markets that lacked direction.

Know that you will have bad days. (Remember Commandment 8: You've got to love your losers like you love your winners.) You must be able to bounce back psychologically the next day (or the day after that) and look at the market and your trading plan with a fresh perspective. Here's what I mean: It's not constructive to say, "Yesterday I lost a lot of money. If I don't make a lot of money today I'm in trouble." (Or worse still, you could put the blame on "them"—other traders, institutions, arbitrageurs, major central banks, economic cartels, your computer, your software program, your parents, your spouse, your dog, the Fed, solar radiation, or your inner child.)

Just like you might be tempted to brag about your big trades, you have to own up to your bad trades. You can't go through life (or trading) blaming someone else for your mistakes. The better way to do this is to say, "[Expletive deleted], I really made some mistakes yesterday that cost me. But I've learned a few things. I had better start out slow today, make some profits, and then move on." Believe me, the latter is a far better mental attitude for success. You'll have a restless night, but in the morning you will be ready for the market to reopen. Then you'll be back in the game—and ready to fight.

Sure, when you're going through the loss, it's very painful. But exiting a losing trade provides a tremendous amount of clarity and even relief in some cases. When you're out of that trade—it's over; that's as bad as it's going to get on that trade. It's not the end of the world if you lose money. It's only a problem if you let those losses eat at you and cloud your judgment.

Once your mind is ready to trade, it's time to focus on the market. In fact, your mental preparation and the study of your indicators and technical analysis, which we will address in depth later in the book, go hand in hand.

When I began trading, I would pore over price charts for an hour every morning, committing the prices on the paper to my memory. Today, my technical review time is compressed. For one thing, as a large, independent trader (or "local," as we're called) I am on the front lines of the market every day. I am literally a part of what appears on that chart. In addition, I employ the services of technicians who provide a synopsis of the market and indicators.

As we'll discuss in upcoming chapters, you cannot devise a trading plan—which governs every trade that you make—without first studying previous market patterns. Looking at such things as previous highs and lows, moving averages, and so forth will help you determine the type of market you're in—whether the stock you've been trading is stuck in a range or the futures market is setting up for a trend reversal.

While I focus on the S&P futures, this methodology of trading will work with any market, whether it's a stock, an equity index futures contract, or commodities. Or, as I'm fond of saying, a trader can trade anything that has enough liquidity and volume. If it has a price that moves, a trader can trade it!

One thing to bear in mind as you read this book: My goal is not to give you the holy grail of trading. First of all, there is no holy grail of trading—and if there were, nobody (including me) would sell it to you for a few dollars. Rather, my goal is to give you some guidance and support as you move along the learning curve of trading. These are the lessons that I, with 20 years' experience as a trader, had to master—and there are some that still challenge me. Let the experience of others help you to shorten your learning curve and offer support when you face a difficulty. Remember, trading is a discipline that is honed.

But there is no substitute for your own hard work. It's your mental discipline that will determine your readiness to trade. It's your technical analysis and homework in the markets that will help you devise a plan. The good news is, you're not in this alone. The goal of this book—and the mission of my web site, TeachTrade.com—is to provide insights for traders from traders, like me.

And with that, let's begin.

2

Getting Started

For day traders of stocks and futures, there is perhaps no better time—technologically speaking—to be in the market than right now. To underscore the point, I'm not talking about market dynamics. And I'm not saying that an individual's chance of success has improved. Rather, the evolution in market access that we've experienced over the past 30 years has led to a democratization of the financial markets. Moving forward, there's no question that this evolution will continue when it comes to direct and equal (or near equal) access to the markets, speed of online execution, and competitive offerings of quotes and market information.

What that means for the trader is that the choices for how to trade have increased. Broker-assisted. Discount brokerage. Online brokerage. Direct access. Those changes are happening in both stocks and futures, although the futures markets to this point have lagged the stocks when it comes to the explosion in online individual participation.

In this chapter, we're going to look at the three basic requirements of any trader for getting started. These three issues comprise the core of your system, whether you're trading at home or in a trading room with other professionals. These requirements are:

1. Brokerage (including commissions and fees)

2. Leverage and capitalization

3. Sources of market information

Because this is an evolving marketplace for the individual trader, it's important to look backward to gain a full appreciation for—and understanding of—where we are today. Equally important, you must understand the changes that have taken place in this marketplace over the past 30 years so you can assess the brokerage and market access that's being offered to you.

First, there was the big bang (not the birth of the universe; the other big bang—the one that deregulated the U.S. stock market). Before this time, high commissions were charged uniformly across Wall Street. For example, if you wanted to buy 1,000 shares of a $50 stock in the early 1970s, it could cost you around $2,500. (Today, by comparison, you can pay as little as one penny per share to buy and sell stock. For 1,000 shares, that means $10 to buy and $10 to sell.)

Those high, across-the-board commissions charged by brokerage houses caught the displeased eye of the Securities and Exchange Commission (SEC) and the Federal Trade Commission (FTC). These agencies' efforts to deregulate commissions and to open the door to competition among brokerages resulted in the big bang, which, while it may not have been as big as the birth of the universe, did create a whole new world for traders.

In 1974, the Securities and Exchange Commission mandated a 13-month trial period during which certain brokerage transactions were deregulated. And it's no coincidence that this same year Charles Schwab started his discount brokerage. Then, on May 1, 1975, the SEC officially approved "negotiated" commissions, which marked the birth of the discount brokerage industry. (Charles Schwab & Co. web site, www.schwab.com, "1975–1977: The Birth of Discount Brokerage.")

A discount brokerage delivered what its name implied. It no longer cost the same price across Wall Street to execute a trade. The launch of the discount brokerage industry brought competition to the cost of buying and selling stock. This was the first step in the leveling of Wall Street's playing field, a trend that would become more dramatic in the 1990s with the explosion in online trading.

But before the Internet and the advent of the "dot-com" trader, there was another significant event that gave the start to stock day trading: the birth of the Nasdaq Small Order Execution System (SOES). The Nasdaq began trading in 1971, some 10 years after the SEC proposed an automated marketplace to be implemented by the National Association of Security Dealers. But Nasdaq, like the rest of Wall Street, was a game with limited players.

That changed with the birth of SOES, which was specifically meant for the execution of orders of 1,000 shares or less. This, in turn, gave rise to SOES trading, enabling the automatic execution of small orders against the best quotations. More important from a day trader's perspective, SOES allowed a new breed of day trader to capitalize on price fluctuations and temporary discrepancies in prices quoted by market makers. Speculation was no longer a gentleman's game on Wall Street. It was in the trenches—fast and sometimes wild.

I was a partner in one of the first SOES rooms in Chicago, where I witnessed a room full of would-be traders clicking their way to riches—or so they hoped. More often than not, the SOES traders in the Chicago trading room saw more losses than gains. Why? At that time, these SOES traders were being charged the full commission of $25 a trade. I argued with my partners to lower commissions to $7, but they would not hear of it. It was the beginning of the end of our partnership.

But for our purposes here, the Chicago SOES room illustrated clearly that average people had the desire to trade and to take on risk. This was not a broker in some white-shoe firm. This was an entrepreneur with guts who made numerous short-term trades to scalp sixteenths and eighths. Cleary, this was "not your father's stock investing," to paraphrase the Oldsmobile slogan. This was a shoot-from-the-hip trader who was buying and selling stocks when the price discrepancy afforded an opportunity. Later, as the prices became more uniform, these traders looked for stock prices that moved. They wanted to buy at 10 and sell hours or even minutes later for $10\frac{1}{4}$ or $10\frac{1}{2}$—over and over again, in hopes of making more money than their commissions and trading costs consumed. They weren't investing. They had even moved beyond traditional stock trading to ultra-short-term trading known as scalping.

On the other side of the financial market lived another breed of scalper—the futures trader. As a young trader myself back in the early 1980s, I did my share of scalping. You waited for a big buy or sell order to hit the pit. There would be a momentary upset in the equilibrium that you could take advantage of. If a big order pushed the market down, you bought at what you thought was the momentary low in hopes of selling out a minute or so later when the price ticked higher. In and out, in and out—all day long in the market, as long as it moved.

Now, remember the history of futures. Midwest farmers who sold their grain at harvest time needed to set a price earlier in the year and raise money in the process. A group of merchants got together and formed a marketplace, which in time would become the foundation of the Chicago Board of Trade. This "future selling" allowed the hedger—in this case the farmer—to meet the speculator. The speculator would agree to buy X number of bushels of grain for a set price, which would be delivered at harvest time. The hedger would be able to lock in a price for his crop. The risk for the speculator was to buy too high. And the risk for the hedger was to sell too low. But the advantage for each was opportunity.

In time, we evolved to financial futures, including currencies, Eurodollars, and stock index futures. But in these markets, the same players meet. For example, in the S&P futures pit where I trade, the hedgers are the institutions with large stock portfolios that need to lay off risk or lock in returns, or perform any number of complex hedging strategies involving stocks, futures, and options. The speculators are those who take the other side of those trades, namely the independent "local" traders like me. We provide the liquidity for those speculators to trade sometimes hundreds or even thousands of contracts. As the buying and selling of contracts ensues the price fluctuates, sometimes with great volatility, which allows others to speculate solely on the movement.

Remember, if a market has volume and liquidity, a trader will trade it. (I used to say a good trader could trade "snow futures" if there were enough volume and liquidity and the price moved enough.) And keep in mind that futures traders were the original day traders. We locals don't buy an S&P contract and hang on to it for five years. We buy and sell all day long, scalping for profits. The vast majority of the time I go home "flat," neither short nor long. On a few occasions I do take a position that will last overnight or occasionally a day or two, but never longer than a few days.

At this point, let's bring these two breeds of speculators together: There is the stock day trader who is looking to make quick profits on momentary fluctuations in stock prices, and there is the futures trader who is day trading in the futures market. They are professionals. They don't have another "day job"—trading *is* their day job (for however long their capital lasts).

Now, fast-forward to the late 1990s, when the Internet and instant access to market information led to a new, hybrid player. They call themselves "day traders," when in fact they're probably better described as "short-term traders." The stock craze has extended beyond these would-be day traders to embrace a more active investing public. About half of all U.S. households—or about 78.7 million people— own stocks.

As share prices rose in the 1990s and the access to information and the marketplace increased, the line between investor and speculator blurred. People who used to buy mutual funds decided to try their hands at doing their own portfolio management by buying stock. Watching their buy-and-hold investments on a daily basis they saw price fluctuations that tempted them to buy and sell quickly. The transition was from investor to active investor to speculator to hybrid day trader.

Unfortunately, many of these day trades were not placed based on technical analysis of the market. Rather, people would buy based on what they saw, heard, or believed—or a tip they got at the health club. They'd buy and they'd wait. The stock would go up because of a prevailing bull market. (Remember 1999? Nasdaq was up 86 percent.) This became so prevalent that many companies banned employees from day trading at their desks.

I got a firsthand view of this phenomenon when I lectured at Hofstra University on Long Island in October 1999. I asked some 200 students or so in a lecture hall how many of them day traded. I expected maybe one or two hands. Half the hands went up! I was later told that students had Internet connections at their desks, which had to be disconnected because they were day trading during class. One student told me that it wasn't uncommon for someone to stand up in the middle of a lecture and shout out, "I just made $1,000 bucks!"

Much has been written about the bonanza of day trading. Yes, there were some "click-quick" millionaires, but more commonly the uninitiated pointed and clicked their ways to ruin. Even dedicated investors who tried their hands at this short-term speculation got burned in the subsequent market downturn in 2000. Margin calls of $25,000, $50,000, or even more were not uncommon. As painful as this correction was for many individuals, looking back you can see there is something wrong with the picture when an amateur trader playing in the market can make more money there than in his or her day job. I know of an orthodontist who had a very successful practice and yet made $2 million by day trading. That clearly was a bubble that was waiting to be burst—as Fed chairman Alan Greenspan had alluded to it in 1999.

I know one sad story of a young man who thought he could day trade his way to wealth for himself and his family. His father, who had worked hard all his life, set him up with a few hundred thousand dollars, which the son quickly blew through. Instead of stopping, the son—and the father—decided they had to make it back. Greed had brought them to this point, and now fear was going to finish them off. By the end of the son's day trading career, his father had to sell his $2 million house to pay for the son's trading losses.

It used to be that a dot-com was virtually guaranteed a high price-to-earnings multiple that would keep rising. But what the investing masses lost sight of was the fact that "what goes up must come down."

Paper fortunes made in stocks evaporated. Consider CMGI, which is trading far below its once-lofty heights. (See Figure 2.1.)

Or consider Yahoo!, which on March 7 saw a 22 percent decline in its stock price after it issued a second earnings warning and said that its chief executive officer (CEO) would step aside "amid a ferocious decline in profit." ("Investors Wallop Yahoo Shares; Earnings Warning, Koogle Removal Take Toll," by Bambi Francisco, CBS Market-Watch.com, March 8, 2001.) Yahoo! as of that date had a 52-week range of $205\frac{5}{8}$ to 17. In April, it would dip below $12 a share. (See Figure 2.2.)

If at this point you are asking yourself why you want to pursue day trading professionally, that's a good thing. The only way to get into trading is with your eyes wide open. You must be aware of the odds

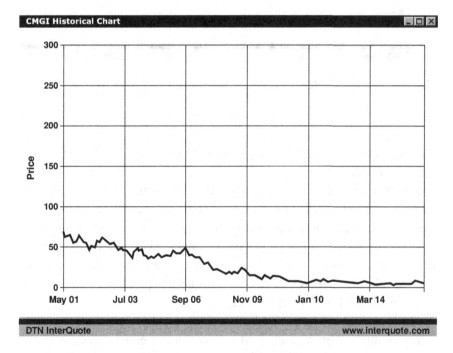

Figure 2.1 CMGI Historical Chart (*Source:* www/interquote.com, DTN Financial Services)

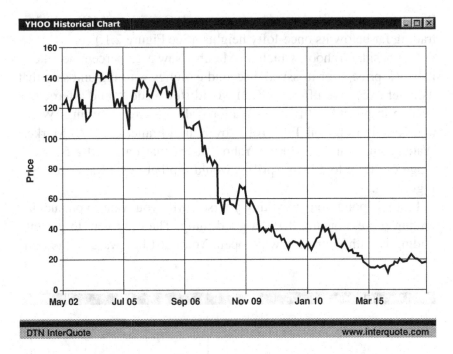

Figure 2.2 YHOO Historical Chart (*Source:* www/interquote.com, DTN Financial Services)

that are stacked against you if you want to play and ever have the possibility of succeeding.

Another thing to keep in mind is that the virtual explosion in day trading sparked another revolution in the brokerages. To attract business, brokerages slashed commissions—sometimes even made offers of *no* commissions—just to get the business. They made their money by taking the other side of some customer orders, by selling the order flow to other brokerages (a common brokerage practice), or on the interest associated with margin trades.

Online order execution in the late 1990s really meant a fast way to e-mail your broker. You clicked on your order entry screen—say, to buy 100 shares of IBM—and then "transmitted" an order. A human being at the other end, however, still had to process the order. But, now, direct electronic access is being offered in the equity and futures markets. For the dedicated, professional trader, direct access speeds your order to the marketplace with a minimum of human and/or electronic intervention. The brokerage that offers direct access has a competitive advantage over one that is still offering only the "fast way to e-mail your broker" service. And, given the downturn in the market that has resulted in a decline in casual day traders, brokerages are scrambling to capture and retain traders.

Take Schwab as an example. On January 30, 2001, Schwab said it was asking "nonessential employees" to take one day off from work on a Friday in February or March as part of an effort to cut costs. ("Schwab to Cut Work Week for Some," by Nicole Maestri, CBS MarketWatch.com.) Then, some six weeks later, Schwab, the number one U.S. discount and online brokerage, said it was offering its customers direct access to stock markets and more extensive stock quotes. The move, Schwab said, was aimed at expanding its "leadership position" with active traders who make more than four trades a month or 48 trades a year. This new service stemmed from Schwab's purchase of CyBerCorp, which catered to stock day traders, about a year before.

Where, you ask at this point, do you fit into all this? Perhaps you've been dabbling in day trading for a few months, or maybe you've just gotten back into it after a few losses that scared you to the sidelines in 2000. Maybe day trading has always appealed to you, and now, after watching the tech sector sink to a low that you believe *must* be the bottom, you want to get in. What does all this have to do with you?

As you start out in day trading you will be one of the most sought after of commodities: fresh blood for the brokerages. You will be enticed with low rates and supposedly surefire systems. That's good news for you as a consumer. The brokerage market is competitive, perhaps more so than ever before given the great strides that firms took to capture retail trading in 1999—and the subsequent downturn they saw in business in 2000 and into 2001.

Don't forget that what has happened to day traders hasn't happened in a vacuum. The retail *investor* market also has seen its share of declines. In February 2001, U.S. investors pulled a record $13 billion out of stock mutual funds, with a total of $5.5 billion in outflows from equity mutual funds in the last five days of February. Keep in mind that huge inflows had contributed to the strength of the bull market over the past two years. Individual investors make up about 40 percent of the money in the stock market. ("U.S. Stock Funds See Record Outflows; Estimated $13 Billion Drop in February Mirrors Concerns," by Craig Tolliver and Trish Regan, CBS MarketWatch.com, March 1, 2001.)

So when you go out looking for a place to park your trading account, you're going to be very popular. You should know that brokerages are looking not only for new accounts, but also to gather assets. Brokerages want to hold your portfolio *and* allow you to trade. Don't forget: If you buy and sell stocks actively—on your own, without a broker's advice—the brokerage can still reap the profits of the commissions, even at discounted rates. And while you buy and sell in and out of securities at your own discretion, brokerages can also avoid that scourge of the business, the appearance of "churning," or turning over portfolio holdings allegedly to collect commissions. Rather, these so-called day traders have been churning themselves, into and out of stocks, and the brokerages have been pocketing the commissions or making money on selling the order flow, which we'll address shortly.

That's why it's imperative that you become aware of what you're getting into before you dive into online trading. Caveat emptor. Or in this case, let the *trader* beware!

You must consider all the options and aspects of your three main requirements for trading, as outlined earlier in the chapter: brokerage; leverage and capitalization; information sources. We'll discuss each of these separately, addressing specific areas for both stocks and futures.

BROKERAGE—STOCKS

When considering a brokerage, most traders and active, short-term investors want to know one thing: What's my commission rate? But price is not the only consideration. Equally (if not more) important are the issues of reliability and ease of use. So don't just look at the bargain-basement price being offered, under $10 per trade or even free under special conditions and promotional events. Understand who is executing your order and how it is being accomplished.

For example, if you have an online stock trading account, you cannot assume that clicking on the "transmit" button will send your order to buy or sell stock directly into the marketplace. Rather, what happens with traditional online trading accounts is that by hitting the "enter" key you send your order via the Internet to your broker. That's why we call this a "faster way to e-mail your broker." At that point, your broker decides which market to send your order to for execution. That's very similar to what happens when you call your broker to place a stock trade.

While this doesn't involve an enormous delay, the process can affect the price of a particular stock. For example, Stock X may have hit your entry level of $20 on your screen, but by the time you transmit your order to your broker and the order is routed to the marketplace and filled, the price could very well be higher—maybe by a quarter or a half point.

Also keep in mind that price quotes are only for a specific number of shares. Therefore, you may not receive the price you see on the screen when you execute your order.

What should you do if you consistently are filled at a significantly different price than what you see on the screen? Here's a tip from the SEC's "Investor Tips" posted on the agency's web site (www.sec.gov). "No SEC regulations require a trade to be executed within a set period of time. But if firms advertise their speed of execution, they must not exaggerate or fail to tell investors about the possibility of significant delays."

For you, the retail short-term trader, that statement once again places the burden of responsibility squarely on your shoulders. Know what you're getting into before you open an online account. Understand that there can be significant delays—and therefore price discrepancies—when you place a trade.

Also keep in mind that your broker has several choices when it comes to executing your stock trade. For example:

- Your broker may direct your order to a major exchange (such as the New York Stock Exchange), to a regional exchange, or to a "third market maker" that buys or sells stocks listed on an exchange at publicly quoted prices. The SEC notes, "As a way to attract orders from brokers, some regional exchanges or third market makers will *pay your broker* [emphasis mine] for routing your order to that exchange or market maker—perhaps a penny or more per share for your order. This is called 'payment for order flow.'"

- For a Nasdaq stock, your broker may send the order to a Nasdaq market maker in that stock. Many Nasdaq market makers also pay brokers for order flow.

- Your broker may route your order—especially a limit order to be transacted at a certain price—to an electronic communications network (ECN) that automatically matches buy and sell orders at specified prices.

- Another option is for your broker to keep the order in-house. This means that your brokerage will take the other side of your order, filling it out of inventory. That allows your brokerage to make money on the spread, the difference between the bid and the ask (also called "offer") price.

Keep in mind, however, that your broker still has a duty to seek the best execution that is "reasonably available" for customers' orders. As the SEC notes, "That means your broker must evaluate the orders it receives from all customers in the aggregate and periodically assess which competing markets, market makers, or ECNs offer the most favorable terms of execution."

If there is a common complaint among novice traders it is that the price they see is rarely the price they get. Rather, they typically buy higher and sell lower than their target prices. The reasons are often twofold. In fast-moving markets, the price can change between the "click" and the fill, particularly if your broker must still examine and route your order. Also, if the brokerage is taking the other side of your order, you may end up buying at the ask or offer and selling at the bid. Remember, a stock is bid (to buy) at one price and is offered (for sale) at another—the ask price. The difference between those

---

Legends, Language, and Lore of Traders

There are times when you're trading either stocks or futures that you just can't get into the market where and when you want to. Let's say you want to be a buyer if a particular stock or futures contract gets above a specific price level. But when it starts to move, it takes off like a rocket. The stock is now $1 or $2 higher than your ideal entry point, or the futures contract is 10 or 20 "handles" higher. (A 10-handle gain in S&P futures would be from 1310 to 1320.)

Every trader has suffered from this frustration. And the danger, which you resist, is chasing the market (i.e., buying well after the uptrend has been established and begins to top out, or selling long after the downturn and the market begins to turn around). If that happens, you can end up with the opposite of what you want: You're buying high and selling low.

There are many days in a trader's life when you're left on the sidelines, unable to capitalize on a move you saw coming because once it started it just steamrollered by. Then, as we'll discuss in upcoming chapters, you take a look at your trade setup and what contributed to you being late on that particular move. Sometimes, it just happens: You can't get in. Your electronic order-entry system goes down. Or the major players are bidding (or offering) so aggressively that smaller players can't get in.

Then remember this: When you're right but the market passes you by, you can congratulate yourself on your ability to spot the trend (albeit it a little late). And know that when you're wrong—and that stock you buy because you think it will rocket higher fizzles instead—you can get all you want.

Such is the life of a trader.

two quotes—which could widen or narrow depending on market conditions—is the spread.

That brings up a particular point for beginning traders. Let's say a stock hits your desired price—it has found support on the downside or an upward move has generated a buy signal. If you place a "market order," you will be filled at the best prevailing market price at that time for your requested amount of shares. If you place a "limit order," you will be filled at the price if it's available for your requested amount of shares. Remember, there is no guarantee that a limit order can be filled, particularly in a fast-moving market. However, that limit order must be filled before the security is allowed to trade through the limit, unless it was an all-or-none (AON) order.

If you're truly day trading—and that means buying and selling hundreds or even thousands of shares of stocks from morning until afternoon—a 25-cent difference in a stock price really matters. Again, if you're buying and holding, then an eighth or a quarter or even a half isn't that much of a difference because you're hoping for potentially a double-digit return in your portfolio. Not so when you're truly day trading. For example, let's say your system generates a buy signal in Company X at $20.25 a share and you think the stock could easily go to $21.50 a share and beyond that to $23. We'll say the stock has baseline support at $20. Its sector (whether technology or financial or whatever) is in favor, and the broad market (Nasdaq, S&P, or Dow) also is positive. If you want to buy at $20.25 but you get filled at $20.50, that's a significant difference known as "slippage"—the difference between the price you saw on the screen and the price at which you're filled. Slippage is a fact of life in trading. You won't—in fact, you can't—get the price on the screen all the time, because markets can move in split seconds. Moreover, you may not be able to get the price you want for the volume of shares you're moving.

At the same time, a $0.25-a-share difference in price can have a major impact on your profit-and-loss statement (P/L) when you're trading hundreds or even thousands of shares of stock for a quick scalp, an ultra-short-term trade lasting minutes or hours. (This is the kind of activity that you'll work up to, not start off at.)

That's why serious stock day traders require direct access. Simply put, direct access allows stock traders to enter their orders directly to the marketplace where they can be viewed and acted upon by a variety of broker-dealers. Direct access originated with the New York Stock Exchange's DOT system and its successor, the Super DOT system, which were direct by-products of the securities industry big bang. The DOT was designed to enable brokers to route their clients' orders directly to the floor of the NYSE. Now—as the securities markets become increasingly democratic—professional retail traders are able to gain direct access to the DOT system through services offered by third-market firms and day trading firms. Once routed to the DOT, however, these orders are executed on the floor of the NYSE.

The Nasdaq, meanwhile, has never had a central trading "floor" per se. Rather, since its inception, the Nasdaq has been a network of dealers that make markets—quoting bids and offers—on stocks listed on the Nasdaq. There are several levels of membership in the Nasdaq, and the higher the level of membership the greater your access to the marketplace. The highest level allows broker-dealers to display their bids and offers under the monikers assigned to their firms, and to interact directly with other market makers.

For retail traders, the most common market access for the Nasdaq is Level II. With a Level II screen you are *not* able to enter your order under your own name—say, "Jsmith"—nor can you interact with the market makers. But you can see what those market makers are doing. You can see the other bids and offers from various brokerages, which helps you to see which securities are the most active—at what price and in what quantity. From this perspective of the Level II inner circle, you can trade with potentially the best knowledge of the current market.

Level II access used to be limited to an inner circle of broker-dealers. (See Figure 2.3.) Now, Level II quotes are very widely disseminated. Once again, this is yet another example of the democratization

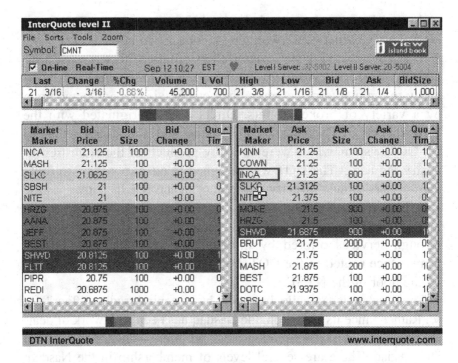

Figure 2.3 InterQuote Level II (*Source:* www.interquote.com, DTN Financial Services)

of the market. Further, it increases the transparency of the market, meaning the bids and offers of the firms—which may very well indicate the short-term trend of a particular security—are available for your viewing.

Viewing firsthand the bids and offers in the market, you can now take advantage of direct-access trading of Nasdaq stocks. With direct access, you do not electronically submit your bid or offer to a broker. Rather, you send it directly to the marketplace via one of several different routes, including ECNs. Among them (in alphabetical order) are:

- Archipelago, which allows users to enter bids and offers into its national book that appears collectively under the ARCA system.

- BRUT ECN, which says it offers "cost-effective and accessible" trading through brokers that subscribe to the system.

- Instinet, which specializes in agency brokerage services to security industry professionals.

- Island ECN, a computerized trading system that allows brokerages to display and match stock orders for retail and institutional investors.

- MarketXT, which provides services to retail brokerages to offer real-time, after-hours trading to individuals.

In essence, the ECNs provide greater order transparency in the marketplace. With an ECN, you can see the bids and the offers, and the number of shares. Remember, with the New York Stock Exchange, large orders from institution to institution—or block orders—are transacted in the "upstairs" office, and then reported after the fact to the NYSE. ECNs allow all participants to see more clearly the buy and sell activity in a particular stock at a particular price.

This combination of ECNs and direct access offered by online brokerages is going to revolutionize the potential for serious retail traders and short-term investors. Of course, to be prudent we must emphasize the word "potential." Direct access does not make trading and short-term investing any less risky. Rather, it carries two potential advantages:

1. Choosing where and how your trades are executed.

2. Speeding your order to the market via direct access, instead of with broker intervention to route your order.

Direct-access trading in equities is offered by a variety of online brokerages. But once again, this is something that active stock traders and investors should graduate to—not start from. In fact, when you are starting out investing there is nothing wrong with the hand-holding that goes with using a full-service broker. You get what you pay for. Investors who need that extra support should seek it out. Eventually, as you become more active, you'll be using online services of the brokerage that will allow you to place a trade automatically. Then, as you become more experienced and you are truly day trading and not just actively investing, you may take advantage of direct access.

Online brokerages that offer direct access have descriptions of this service and the usual disclaimer-caveats that go with them. In summary, here are some important considerations for direct-access trading of equities.

- Direct access allows you, in effect, to become your own order desk, routing orders to specific exchanges or ECNs. To do this effectively, however, you must learn how to find the liquidity for the stock you are trading in a given market.

- Direct-access software also allows you to see Level II pricing, revealing the activity—the bids and offers—of the market makers. Aggressive buying or selling in a particular equity could be an indication of a short-term trend. Moreover, when a trader enters an order and it does not get filled immediately, he or she can see, via the Level II, why it is not getting filled—the prevailing market prices are far above the trader's bid or below the ask. And the trader can cancel that order and enter a new one that could be more attractive to buyers or sellers.

Another potential advantage is that, with direct access, traders can see the spread on a Level II window and, potentially, capture it for themselves—depending on the market activity in a given stock at the time. With online trading, brokers may sell the order flow or execute it from their own "book" of customer orders, with the brokerage making a profit on the spread.

Keep in mind that neither online trading nor direct access is any better than the other. Rather, they tend to appeal to different trading styles. Online trading may be most suited to those short-term traders who hold positions for a few days or even weeks. Those who are truly day traders, holding a position for *no longer than a day* (and often just minutes or a few hours) may find that direct access gives them a greater advantage when it comes to price.

However, it cannot be stressed too much that direct-access trading is not for the uninitiated. Before you consider direct access you must be experienced in stock trading, and you must educate yourself on various aspects of the market, from the differences between the various ECNs to watching activity on the Level II for indication of a market trend. Put another way, as a direct-access trader, you not only have more control over how your trade is executed, you also have complete responsibility for it. Keep in mind the lessons of Chapter 1: When you have responsibility for your trades, you own your losses, as well as your wins. You don't blame the broker or the marketplace or the sun's glare on your computer screen for your unprofitable trades. You and you alone initiate the trade and live with the result.

BROKERAGE—FUTURES

The evolution of online trading of futures has mirrored that of stocks. But online futures trading has not seen the explosion in the retail market that stocks have. For one thing, there needs to be greater education in the retail market about the use of futures, including their use as a complement to a stock-trading strategy. However, as we'll discuss later in this chapter, there are some definite advantages to be considered with futures trading when it comes to leverage and margin.

But before we go further, let's take a look at the various brokerage options available to a retail futures trader. When you're starting out, it's probably best to phone your broker to place your orders. Using a full-service broker—and paying a full-service commission—during the start of your learning curve gives you some hand-

holding on order execution. Depending on the services offered by
your broker, you may be able to discuss your order with a broker.
More experienced and active traders may be able to place a call
right to the order desk, where it is passed immediately to a broker in
a pit for execution.

Keep in mind that in futures there is no "off-sides" trading—
meaning that the broker doesn't have the option of taking the other
side of your order, as exists in stocks. Rather, when you want to
trade futures, you must go to the exchange in one form or another.
Most futures contracts are now electronically accessible. However,
there is a very important distinction between electronically accessed
and electronically traded.

With electronic access, you are able to send your bid or offer to a
broker electronically, much like traditional online stock trading. Your
order, however, is received by a broker who must then execute it (as
we'll discuss momentarily).

In an electronically traded market, however, your order goes
directly to an electronic trading platform. There, the best bids
and offers are matched and the trades executed. There is no
human intervention once you transmit your order into this electronic venue.

For our purposes in this book, we'll discuss S&P futures based on
the S&P 500 cash index and the Nasdaq based on the Nasdaq 100. As
futures contracts, they are based on the underlying value of the index
and have a cash settlement. During the trading day—from 8:30 A.M.
until 3:15 P.M. Central time—the S&P and the Nasdaq are traded only
in the pit, via open outcry, at the Chicago Mercantile Exchange (the
Merc). (The comparatively less active Dow futures contract trades at
the Chicago Board of Trade.)

For those of you who are not familiar with a futures exchange, a
pit is like a small arena with tiered steps all the way around. On the
top step, at floor level, stand the brokers. They have direct eye
contact with brokers at order desks around the trading floor, who
flash customer orders to them using an elaborate system of hand
signals. Or orders that are transmitted electronically may be displayed on handheld computers that brokers use in the pit. They con-

stantly check their order-display screens for the time, price, and quantity of the customer bids and offers, and then execute the orders in the pit.

To execute their orders—whether it's a 10-lot from a retail customer or an institution wanting to buy or sell a few hundred S&P major contracts—the brokers rely on the independent traders, or "locals," like me. We stand in the next tiers of steps, and the closer to the brokers the better. In an open-outcry environment, proximity is everything. If you can't see or hear the brokers, you won't get the business.

When the pit is full, there are some 500 screaming, shouting, and hyperactive traders and brokers bidding and offering in a system that is aptly named "open outcry." You shout out your bid or your offer, and either someone takes the other side of it or you must adjust your price until you're "hit." The transactions are recorded by the Merc and become the prevailing price at any given moment.

The S&P and Nasdaq futures contracts were primarily designed to be speculative instruments that would allow portfolio managers to lay off—or hedge—some of the risk from their stock holdings. In the simplest of terms, a portfolio manager with a $5 million portfolio with a 20 percent gain may want to lock in that return by hedging in the S&P market. The value of the S&P is 250 times the index. If S&P futures are at 1300, that means one contract has a face value of $325,000. By selling some 5, 10, or 15 contracts, a portfolio manager would be short the S&P for an amount equal to a portion or virtually all the portfolio value. This short futures position would be profitable should the market go down, and offset losses in the stock portfolio.

But one contract worth a few hundred thousand dollars is a pretty big bite for a retail trader/speculator to take. So the Merc launched a scaled-down version of the S&P contract known as the S&P mini, which has one-fifth the value of the S&P major. Thus if the S&P major traded in the pit is worth $325,000, the e-mini would be worth about $65,000. The value of the contract at a particular time is based on the index price, which fluctuates as futures trade. Similarly, there is also an e-mini Nasdaq contract.

These e-mini contracts trade electronically via the Merc's proprietary Globex system. Originally, Globex was used only for after-hours trading. For the S&P and Nasdaq major contracts, the Globex is still used after hours. But during the day, if you want to trade S&P e-minis, for example, your orders will be executed on the Globex terminal.

When you're starting out trading, you can still call your broker to buy, for example, two S&P e-minis. That bid is then entered by your brokerage firm into the Globex. (Some professional trading firms, such as mine, have their own Globex terminals as well.) When your order goes to the Globex server, it is not touched by a broker. Rather, it is matched with another order, all on the basis of time and price.

This electronic access and the scaled-down size of the e-minis have made them extremely popular with retail traders/speculators. By the same token, most online futures traders use the e-minis to take advantage of the electronic access and the scaled-down value (see "Capitalization—Futures" later in this chapter).

In futures, electronic trading is no longer an option, but rather a necessity. While you may start out using a broker to assist you in your orders, serious retail traders will want to graduate to electronic trading. Your goal, therefore, is to be comfortable and adept at electronic trading. In time, the future of futures trading will be electronic. Yes, a hybrid of open-outcry and electronic trading—in my opinion—will exist. But if you want to trade futures, you had best learn your way around electronic order execution.

Let's put it this way: Four years ago, some 5 percent of all futures trading was done electronically. Now the figure is around 25 percent. The advantages of electronic trading are obvious: It's quicker than phoning your broker and eliminates the potential for human error along the way to your order being executed. Plus, a platform like the Merc's Globex is based on time and price, which creates a very fair marketplace.

But there are potential disadvantages, too. One is your own error, whether you click on "bid" when you really mean "offer" or you enter a price or quantity incorrectly. Or you could face system problems and shutdowns. Whether it's your Internet connection or your broker's electronic system, it's important to know that electronic trading systems can and will break down. Knowing that will happen occasionally will not only help you to deal with the frustration, but remind you to have a backup plan when it does. If you are going to trade electronically, be sure you have a phone backup—a telephone number and a contact name—so if you can't enter your orders online you can call your broker to place your trades. This is especially important if you are exiting a position.

When it comes to electronic trading, virtually every futures clearing merchant (FCM) offers an electronic order-entry platform. For example, ED&F Mann and Refco, two of the largest FCMs, between them offer several order-execution platforms, depending on a trader's needs, experience, and other qualifying criteria.

In general, the platforms are either application-based or browser-based. Application-based platforms require you to download the software onto your computer. The program for trading resides on your hard drive and, using this program, you can execute online orders. This is especially important for traders who have a slow Internet connection.

With the browser-based platform, you access the software from the broker's server via the Internet. Every time you issue a command, you are essentially going to the broker's server, retrieving something or enabling a function, going back to your computer, and then executing it. Obviously, you need a fast Internet connection to utilize the browser-based platform.

Whatever platform you use, when you enter a futures order electronically, there is no human intervention per se. You essentially have direct access to the electronic futures marketplace, better known as the Globex server. Your order is transmitted from your computer to the server at the FCM, which usually has a risk-management software application embedded in it. This risk program basically ensures that you have enough capital in your account to cover the trade you're making. After this clearance, which takes about one second to transpire, your

order is sent to the Globex terminal, where it becomes part of the bids
and offers displayed on the screen. When the trade is executed, a confirmation of the "fill" is transmitted back to you.

Typically, it takes only a few seconds from the transmission of a
market order to execution on Globex. Receipt of the confirmation may
take longer—perhaps 20 seconds. But the most important leg of that
electronic journey—from transmission to filling of the order—should
take no longer than five seconds.

As with online stock trading, the most important consideration
is reliability, followed closely by ease of use. Price is a consideration, but it's not the number-one deciding factor. And all too often
what looks like a good deal may not be such a bargain on closer
examination.

When evaluating brokerage commissions for futures trading, remember that the standard is to quote prices per roundturn, in and out
of the position. Also, certain clearing fees and other costs are tacked
onto the commission, such as Globex fees and National Futures Association (NFA) fees for S&P and Nasdaq e-mini commissions. Before
you sign any account forms, make sure you understand the commission rate structure:

- What is the commission rate *per roundturn*?

- What fees will be applied in addition to the commission?

- What are the rates for other futures contracts you might want to
  trade? For example, a brokerage may have a low "special" rate
  for one contract, but other contracts could be subject to a
  higher rate.

LEVERAGE AND CAPITALIZATION

When it comes to opening an electronic trading account—either in
stocks or in futures—one of the most common questions asked is,

"How much money do I need?" Before you get to the absolute dollar amount, there are several considerations. Truly you cannot underestimate the risk involved in day trading both stocks and futures, particularly in the early stages of the learning curve. As stated in Chapter 1, you should not expect to make a profit—other than covering your costs—the first year. Therefore, the money you commit to day trading should be speculative capital. Whatever the amount—from $5,000 to $50,000 or more—you have to know that if you lost every penny of it, your livelihood or your standard of living would not be affected. In other words, don't use next month's mortgage payment or all your retirement savings.

Once you make an honest appraisal of the amount of money that you can put at risk, compare that to the requirements of the brokerage firms that you're investigating.

Stocks—Capital Requirements

When it comes to trading stocks, you have to look at margin requirements. Margin is like a short-term line of credit from your broker based on the amount of capital in your account. Under SEC regulations, a retail stock trader with a margin account can take advantage of 2-to-1 leverage. In other words, if you want to buy 100 shares of a $50 stock, you could either pay out $5,000 directly or you could put up $2,500 and borrow the other $2,500 from the brokerage. This is known as buying on margin.

Margin can be a useful thing when it comes to extending your capital. But remember, this is a loan—one that has to be repaid. The brokerage firm is not giving you money or buying half of the stock (and shouldering half the loss or taking half the profit). Keep in mind, however, that any gains—or losses—on that stock position are based on the full $5,000, not just the $2,500 you invested up front.

This 2-to-1 leverage for retail investors has been extended to as much as 10-to-1 at day trading firms over the past 10 years. More typically, this leverage is 6-to-1. This expanded leverage enables day traders to handle larger positions or more frequent positions than their capital would normally allow. But given the volatility of the market and the plights of many day traders who suffered losses as stock prices plummeted in 2000 and early 2001, it's easy to see how this leverage could be as hurtful as helpful for undisciplined traders.

Let's say you open an account at a day trading firm with $25,000 and, for the sake of illustration, you are given 10-to-1 leverage. Now that $25,000 can be traded like $250,000. But keep in mind, your profits and losses are predicated on $250,000—*not* the $25,000 in your account.

With $250,000 to day trade, you could carry on an intraday basis several thousand shares of stock, perhaps encompassing four or five different positions. But this is only for intraday trading. All firms have dynamic risk-management systems to keep you from violating their parameters. So if you carry a position beyond intraday you'll be faced with a margin call, which is basically the demand for more money to be put into your account to cover your stock exposure.

Interestingly, there are stock day-trading firms that encourage traders to get a National Association of Securities Dealers (NASD) Series 7 license. This accomplishes two things: Going through the Series 7 process, including courses, studying, and an exam, a trader demonstrates a knowledge of the market and of the risks involved. That helps to protect the day trading firm, and presumably the day trader as well. The enticement for getting that Series 7, however, is that the trader may qualify for professional leverage.

The leverage being extended to retail traders is another example of the privileges of a few being made accessible to the many. Years ago, only floor members and professional traders would be able to take advantage of expanded leverage. Now qualifying retailer traders—who are deemed by their brokerages to have enough experience and capital—can have leverage of 6-to-1 or more for intraday trades.

Capitalization—Futures

When it comes to capitalization for trading futures, the basic requirements are set by the Chicago Mercantile Exchange, where the S&P and Nasdaq contracts trade, and are enforced by the Commodity Futures Trading Commission (CFTC). The capitalization requirements apply to all members—"local" traders, brokers, and clearing firms. At their own discretion clearing firms can ask for more capital from their clients; however, they must adhere to these minimums.

Currently, the requirement is $4,750 to trade one e-mini contract overnight. So, typically most firms require a minimum of $5,000 to open a futures account. If you intend to day trade and not carry a position overnight, you can typically trade twice the value of your account. Using the $5,000 example, you'd be able to trade two e-minis during the day, and then carry one e-mini overnight.

If you exceeded that limit and carried, for example, two e-minis overnight, you would face a margin call for money to be put into the account. If you failed to do that, the clearing firm would liquidate your position.

Keep in mind that the amount of capital discussed here is the *minimum* requirement. Many firms ask for more, and should ask for more. Far too many traders are undercapitalized. Without a cushion of adequate capital for their trading, they have too much risk and are taken out of the game too early, before they have progressed on the learning curve.

Beyond this, keep in mind that futures are leveraged instruments. This increases the power of your capital, but it also heightens the size of your losses. For example, with a minimum of $5,000 in your account, you could trade two S&P e-minis—worth an aggregate of $130,000 (if the index is at 1300)—intraday. That's 26-to-1 leverage. Your losses and gains are predicated on that $130,000—not the $5,000 in your account. So be aware of the power of leverage when you trade futures. It can work for you—or against you.

This leverage, comparatively low margin requirements, and low-

---

Legends, Language, and Lore of Traders

"S&Ps had a 10-handle range." "Goldman bought 50 cars." Sounds like a foreign language.

Granted, the terminology used in futures trading is not as intuitive as that used in stock trading. In stocks, you buy 1,000 shares or you short 500. It's all self-explanatory.

To bring the uninitiated up to speed in futures-speak, here's a brief glossary:

Points: S&Ps move in increments of 10 points. A point is one-hundredth of a unit. So, from 1100.00 to 1100.10 is 10 points. From 1100 to 1101 would be 100 points.

Handle: A handle equals 100 points. From 1100 to 1101 is one handle. From 1100 to 1102 is two handles.

Cars: Undoubtedly this came from the agrarian days of futures trading, with commodities like live cattle that were shipped in railroad cars. Butter was originally traded at the Chicago Merc (which was first known as the Butter and Egg Board) in units of "car lots." A carload in those days was 19,200 pounds of butter, according to the Merc's web site ("Web Instant Lessons," www.cme.com). In broader futures trading terms, a car is synonymous with a contract. So if Goldman Sachs, for example, was a buyer of "50 cars" in the S&P pit, what that means is Goldman bought 50 S&P contracts.

---

cost commissions can make futures a better deal than equities. What you trade, of course, will depend largely on your preference and your understanding. But even if you intend to trade stocks exclusively, you will need, at a minimum, to be aware of the movements of the stock index futures. Further, you may find that trading stock index futures—in addition to stocks—can help dedicated, professional traders to put more market tools at their disposal. In addition, profits from futures trading are taxed at a blended rate reflecting short-term and long-term capital gains. This is a more favorable tax treatment than that applied to stock trading profits, which are taxed as short-term capital gains and potentially at the highest rate.

Table 2.1 provides a quick glance at the requirements for trading stocks and futures, and a comparison of capitalization, margin, and leverage.

INFORMATION SOURCES

The final consideration when you're getting started trading is your source of information, both real-time price quotes and news headlines. Ideally, you should have two independent sources of real-time quotes. (Remember, unless you're a long-term investor, the delayed price quotes available on many business news web sites are not usable.)

Real-time data and charting packages are widely available from a variety of sources, accessible via the Internet or satellite dish. Given

Table 2.1 Stocks and Futures Trading Requirements

Instrument	Brokerage	Capitalization and Margin	Tax Treatment
Stocks	Online and direct-access trading available. Competitive commission rates under $10 available for qualified traders.	A 50 percent margin is required for stock trades (i.e., a $50,000-stock purchase requires $25,000 in margin held in your account). Professional day traders may be offered 6-to-1 or as high as 10-to-1 leverage by trading firms.	Short-term capital gains from stock trading are taxable at potentially the highest rate.
Futures	Online and direct-access trading available. Low commissions of $10 per roundturn (plus fees) available.	With $5,000 in your account, you can trade two S&P e-minis intraday, worth a total of $130,000—or 26-to-1 margin.	Futures trading profits are taxed at a blended rate reflecting short-term and long-term capital gains.

the fact that even the best Internet service can and will go down (and a host of errors can be generated by routers and servers en route), you must have two sources of data. Imagine you have a trade on and you're watching your screen. You're nearing the price at which you intend to exit. Suddenly your quotes vanish or don't update. In a panic you try to restore quote service, but meanwhile your profitable trade could turn into a loser. Or you could get out of the trade sight unseen and miss out on executing your trade according to your plan for the maximum profit potential.

Data vendors usually provide charting software that will enable you to display the price quotes graphically. As we discuss in upcoming chapters, these real-time price charts will be the map you use to guide your trading, based on the trend lines, moving averages, and other indicators that you apply.

As with most things, data and charting services and software come in a variety of levels of sophistication and pricing. Basic data and charting are available for about $100 a month. Or it's possible to get more in-depth charting and software that allows you to program your own trading system, based on your trading parameters, for thousands of dollars. If you're starting out, it's probably best to get your feet wet with a basic system that doesn't overwhelm or confuse you, and then build up based on your criteria.

The other source of information, of course, is news. You need to know what's going on real-time because events and announcements can and will affect the markets that you're trading. A surprise rate cut by the Federal Reserve can send the equities markets skyrocketing. An earnings warning by a large technology company can send the market plummeting. In between all the surprises, there is a host of regularly scheduled announcements and events.

Among them are earnings announcements and economic releases (see Resources); a calendar of economic events is available on almost any brokerage web site. In addition, stock traders may want to peruse the research made available on brokerage firms' web sites. Moreover, if you're actively trading a stock, you'll want to know when the company is going to release earnings announcements as well as any analyst conference calls scheduled on the company.

Increasingly, companies are managing the release of information about their earnings expectations and their growth prospects. As we've seen throughout the fourth quarter of 2000 and the first quarter of 2001, earnings warnings produce the most dramatic reactions in the market. The actual earnings release is typically a nonevent, unless some other nuance about future growth (or lack thereof) is disclosed.

Ultimately, for day traders and those who want to become serious short-term speculators, it's important to know the minimum requirements for entering this highly competitive arena. Remember, the playing field is populated by professionals (who were once as green as you are!) and institutions that are buying and selling the same stocks and futures contracts that you are. That doesn't mean that you'll be automatically shut out of the game. Rather, you need to give yourself the best advantage possible to compete.

3

Technical Analysis 101

I remember when I was a young order filler standing in the trading pit. When the market hit a certain price level, there would suddenly be a rush of orders. Or there were resting orders above or below the market that were surprisingly close together. What were these people seeing? This was the early 1980s, and futures trading was largely a pit-dominated endeavor. Those who traded off the floor did so through a broker. Online trading as we know it now was unheard-of at that time. And even the retail explosion in stock trading would still be years away.

So the mystery for me in those days was what those other traders—the institutions and the big retail speculators—were seeing. There was another funny thing about those orders that were in my deck (as the stack of market orders—sells on one side and buys on the other—is called). Some customers were almost always right and some were almost always wrong.

As for me, I was a scalper in those days, with no market opinion of my own. I had learned to take advantage of the momentary disruptions in market equilibrium when a big order hit the pit, in hopes that I might make a few ticks as the market righted itself. That's the way it was until I learned about technical analysis. I even studied W. D. Gann, the legendary chartist, whose ideas of price, time, and momentum became part of my own trading rationale. In fact, I was part of a group of traders who bought the original rights to Gann's charts.

Whether you're looking at a price chart for the first time or you've been at this for a while, there is something you must always keep in mind. The past will tell you something about the future. The charts contain the past, whether it's one tick ago or several years ago. Spread out before you, you can see where the market has been. When studied, that can give you some valuable insights into where the market is likely headed, once you have identified patterns that then lead to projections.

Eventually I hired technicians to work for me. I figured they could do what they did best, in their case technical analysis, and I could concentrate on what I did best, which was trade execution. In the early days, I employed a runner who would bring the latest updates to me in the pit from the technicians who worked for me in an upstairs office. Then we used pagers to alert me to call upstairs for updates, and later alphanumeric pagers to transmit the latest trading signals from the charts. Now, with special wireless headsets, the trading floor is connected with offices upstairs, and vice versa.

Regardless of whether you subscribe to a trading system that generates buy and sell signals or you do it completely on your own, you must understand the concept of technical analysis. A price chart is like a trail of footprints of where the market has been, which can be used as a guide to help predict where it's likely to go next.

A chart is a picture to some and a story to others. However you view it, it shows the changes in the perception of value of a stock or index based on where trades are made. A trade occurs when a buyer and a seller agree on specific price at a specific time. A chart, therefore, shows the unfolding of perceptions among buyers and sellers. The study of those charts then is used to forecast future trends based on how buyers and sellers acted at previous price levels.

Remember, technical analysis is not an exact science. It's a lot like getting an X ray or a CAT scan. Taking the images is not that complicated. But interpreting them is where the expertise lies. Similarly, in trading much will be left to your own interpretation, which also reflects your trading style and your trading parameters. And it's possible for two traders to look at the same chart and draw different conclusions, once again based on their trading systems.

The goal of technical analysis for any trader is to identify a trend in the early stage, to stay with that trend until it is near its end, and to exit a trade profitably before or just after the trend reverses. It doesn't matter whether that trend lasts several months, a few days, or a matter of minutes.

Technical analysis is predicated on two basic assumptions. The first is that everything is reflected in the market price, meaning all the factors that make up the perceptions of buyers and sellers. That means supply and demand—whether of a specific product or within an industry sector—as well as fundamental issues such as the breakup value of a company, future revenue and earnings, and the overall growth rate (or lack thereof) of the economy.

The other assumption is that the market moves in trends—up, down, and sideways in a trending range. Further, it's assumed that once a trend is established, the market is more likely to continue that trend than to reverse—that is, until it meets a force that turns it the other way, or until the conditions that established that trend (such as aggressive buyers) no longer exist.

Technical analysis looks for patterns to repeat themselves. Human beings who acted a certain way under a certain set of circumstances are likely to act (or react) the same way when those circumstances resurface. There is a very real, tangible human element to the market. As we discussed in Chapter 1, your goal as a trader is to remove your own emotions and ego from your personal trading equation. But the market is a broad arena with many participants, including institutions trading huge amounts of capital, other professional traders who—like you—are studying the charts and making trading decisions, and the investing public at large that does tend to act very emotionally. This emotional element is one of the reasons the market can sometimes move from overbought to oversold without much equilibrium in between.

The study of technical analysis begins with a chart or a series of charts of whatever stock or market you're trading. It's not uncommon for an experienced trader to look at multiple charts, with varying time frames, of several key stocks and broader market indexes, such as the S&Ps, the Nasdaq, and the Dow. As we begin this preliminary study of technical analysis—regardless of your prior experience—start with a chart of whatever stock or index interests you. You may use intraday or daily charts, depending on whether you want to see the very short-term dynamics or the broader market trends (or both). Bar charts that show the opening and closing level for that bar time frame (whether it's one minute, five minutes, or a whole day) are widely used. Another popular chart format is the candlestick chart, which typically has vertical "bodies" that show the difference between the open and close of that time frame, as well as the extensions above and below. Candlesticks are shaded one color when the market closed higher than it opened for that time period, and another color when it closed lower than it opened.

Whatever chart style or time frame you use—and regardless of what market you're analyzing—the basic techniques apply. Most importantly, you need to train yourself to observe—without emotion and without expectation—what the chart displays. Your ultimate goal then becomes to apply these observations, using a variety of indicators, to determine and confirm the prices at which you would buy and the prices at which you would sell.

One of the technicians I've worked with over the years is Jim Sebanc, a longtime student of the market. He spends his days watching multiple screens that are scrawled with colored indicator lines. A casual observer would probably look at those screens and see chaos. When Jim looks at the screens, he is looking for clues as to what might happen next, and sees the chart patterns and indicators as "artwork." Jim recalls seeing a chart in a brokerage office when he was a teenager and feeling an affinity and sense of enormous potential. He had an instant connection with this visual representation of the market that showed the peaks the market had climbed and the valleys, or dips, where it had declined.

Jim's first trade was to buy stock in what was then Eltra Corp. He made a 50 percent return in 10 months based on what he saw on a chart and thought, "This is what I'm going to do for a living."

He sold at what then became the high of the stock for years, which may have been mostly beginner's luck, Jim recalls. But the price was picked based on the charts.

Today, when Jim starts to explain technical analysis to someone else who is interested in learning, he starts with the observation that most people seem to make a common mistake (not just in this field but in many others). They want the end result *now*, instead of realizing that this is a process of many steps. He then relates this common mistake to the analogy of constructing a building: Some people are so focused on furnishing the penthouse apartment that they neglect to find the lot on which to construct the building!

To Jim, the best way to begin technical analysis is to start with a chart of prices. The first step is to change the amount of data in that chart by adjusting the horizontal and/or vertical scale. Then, just look at the chart with no expectations until you start to relate to the different patterns. Don't try to get the total answer at this point. Don't jump ahead. Just follow what is on the chart. You simply observe what emerges.

Eventually, you will get a sense of when the patterns are completed (such as when—and why—a move will stop or stop and reverse). This method can be applied to any chart on anything that is traded—an individual stock, a futures contract, a commodity, an option, and so forth—and any time frame. As long as it trades and a chart can be produced, the same basic methods of technical analysis will apply. The purpose of this chapter is to give you an overview of technical analysis and the initial steps to devise and implement your trading system. Entire books have been written on some of the topics that will be addressed here briefly!

If there is one lesson to take away from this entire chapter, it is that technical analysis is as much art as science. Don't expect to find just one formula for determining whether the market will go up or down. Rather, you will use a number of indicators to help you gauge the market's direction. At times these indicators, or signals, will be conflicting. Other times, they will mostly be in agreement. That is why you cannot rely on one indicator alone. Rather, you must use a variety of tools to help you with the task of analyzing the market.

The first tool is a chart—any chart, whether it's of a stock, a particular stock index, or a commodity. When you look at a chart such as Figure 3.1, you can see a pattern that resembles a cross section of a mountain range. Mountains go up to a peak and then decline to a valley. When you go up one side of a mountain, you would expect that the other side should be roughly symmetrical.

In this discussion of chart patterns we use the term "symmetry" a little loosely. In certain cases, the pattern may truly be symmetrical—an incline, a peak, and a decline so that the chart pattern resembles an isosceles triangle standing on its base.

For example, examine the symmetry of the pattern in the chart from September 2000 through February 2001, with the "peak" above 1500 in September 2000. You can see a very close symmetry both in time and in price—a fairly slow and steady rise to the high in September,

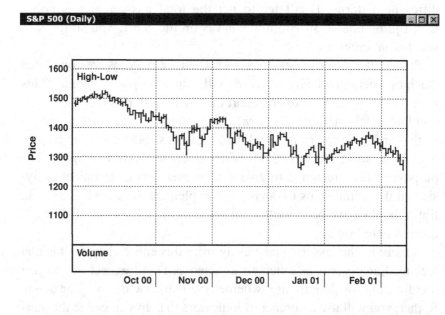

Figure 3.1   S&P 500 I (Daily) (*Source:* www.dtnfs.com, DTN Financial Services)

and then a slightly faster but equivalent drop to October. Another example of this symmetry is the January 2001 move up, followed by a decline in February 2001.

More frequently, however, this symmetry is in time *or* in price (although the pattern may look asymmetrical). For example, with "time symmetry," it takes roughly the same amount of time for a move up and then a move down—up one month (week, day, or hour) and down the same amount of time. However, the price from which the up move started and the price at which the down move ended are at different levels. In "price symmetry," the market may move faster on the ascent or the decline, but the move begins and ends at equivalent price points (e.g., up 50 points in one month and down 50 points in one week).

Also, keep in mind that this symmetry may not be on a horizontal line, but rather on a line that slopes upward—or downward—depending on the general trend.

If at this point you're lost or don't see the connection, then go back and start over. Just look at the chart again, with no expectations of what you might see. Observe the patterns made by the chart. If you don't like the mountain-range analogy, consider waves at the ocean. In fact, ocean waves may be more related to the market since they are dynamic. Sets of waves come into shore—both larger and smaller waves; then there's a lull with very few waves, and then another set. In addition, there's an incoming tide and an outgoing tide, during which the waves will be different. If you study this long enough, you may be able to predict, with some accuracy, the general pattern of the incoming waves. That's what experienced surfers do. They wait for the next set of waves to get the best possible ride. Similarly, your ultimate goal as a trader is to read the charts, just as the surfers read the waves, to help you predict low-risk, high-probability trades.

Once you have made this connection with the chart and can identify the patterns and symmetry, you will have some sense of pattern completion. At this point, it's time to take the next step. Looking at the chart, mark where you'd buy and where you'd sell. Don't just mark "buy" at the bottom and "sell" at the top. Look for the trend reversals and the confirmations to take action. This may seem easy, of course, because you have the advantage of hindsight. (Don't skip this step, either, because you think it's simplistic. Complete each of the suggested steps in this exercise. Remember, one of the attributes all traders need is patience. You have to wait for the market to set up. You can't hurry the market along.)

Once you've marked the buys and sells looking at the entire chart, it's time for the next step. This one is a lot harder since it approximates reading a chart while the market is live.

Get a different chart and cover it completely with a sheet of paper. Now slowly move the covering sheet to the right until you can see some of the chart on the left. Continue moving the covering sheet until the chart reveals what appears to be a buy or a sell signal. Mark that place. Now move the cover sheet further to the right, exposing more time and price. As you examine more of the chart, how well did you do in picking your buy or sell? What would you do differently now since you didn't have the benefit of hindsight?

Continue all the way across the chart, marking the buy and sell signals as they appear to you. When the entire chart is uncovered, look at how well—or how poorly—you did in determining your signals (the lows where you'd buy and the highs where you'd sell).

Repeat this exercise with different charts and different time frames (i.e., daily charts and intraday charts of varying time periods) until you become comfortable with this process in terms of both your understanding and your proficiency.

In addition to marking your buys and sells, also determine where you'd place your "stop." A stop is the point at which you would exit a losing position with a predetermined loss. Thus, if you're buying (going long) you'd place your stop below your entry point in case the market declined. If you're selling (going short) you'd place your stop above your entry point in case the market rallied.

When you pick buys and sells on a chart, part of the decision process is based on patterns of previous highs, lows, and consolidations (congested areas where the market spends a notable amount of time), which are known as resistance and support. Resistance is a price level at which an upward move tends to stall or stop (think of a ceiling). Support is a price level at which a downward move tends to stall or stop (think of a floor). And as every beginning trader quickly learns, a price level that is resistance on the way up then turns into support after the price level is breached and the market moves higher. Similarly, a support level will turn into resistance when the market moves below it. (Think of a multistory building. A level can be a floor or a ceiling, depending on whether your apartment is above or below.)

In the simplest of market terms, let's say a stock is declining and right now is at $50 a share. Suppose there is a previous high on the chart at $45, and very little activity between $50 and the $45. In that case, $45 is now support and a target on a down move. If you are short (and you are a short-term trader), that would be where you would cover that short or at least reduce your position since the stock would likely stop there for the short-term. Conversely, if you are a short-term trader with a long position, and the stock is at $60 with a previous low at $65, that price would be resistance and a price at which to exit or reduce your long position, as the stock should stop there in the short term, and the low risk is over.

Because of their nature, these previous highs, lows, and consolidations tend to attract a lot of attention. In some instances, these levels act like magnets, attracting the buying and selling activity in the market. In a downtrend, for example, markets often will aim for one support level and, if that is breached, will head for the next lower level. Or, on the upside, if the market breaks through one resistance level, it heads for the next higher level.

Remember, the market is always moving. Even when a market is described as "sideways"—meaning it's trading within a tight price range over time—it's still moving. There will be variations in price, however slight, that will make small peaks and valleys on a chart within a broader picture of a sideways market.

Thus, as you study a chart, initially you are looking for the picture that it makes—sharp up and down moves of a mountain, a more gradual rise and decline like a hill, or a plateau made by an up move, a sideways move, and then a down move. Then you will correlate that picture with the actual price levels, identifying where the market made previous highs and previous lows. Using these basic support and resistance price levels, you have the rudiments of technical analysis.

Identifying price patterns is part of the foundation of technical analysis. Most people who don't learn this part are the impatient types who want the answers now without doing the work. When they then try to develop indicators, they look only for static buy and sell signals, instead of reading the dynamics that generate the buy and sell signals. Therefore, they usually become very emotional and animated when things go against their positions, and spend more time in frustration than in developing their understanding. To avoid that pitfall, focus on this first part of technical analysis, which will help you to develop an understanding of the dynamic structure of market. Without this basic understanding, each progressive step may become more confusing and more difficult. (And if you're still in doubt, go back to Chapter 1 and read the Ten Commandments of Trading.)

When you have a true understanding of the price patterns—enabling you to look at a chart and actually see something meaningful—then you can begin the next step, which is developing indicators. Indicators are measurements to help you gauge a variety of factors, including trend, momentum, volatility, and velocity.

The first indicators to start with, and the simplest to understand, are moving averages. Simply put, the moving average is an average of prices over a specific period of time, whether it's 200 days, 50 days, 10 days, or, on an intraday chart, 200 minutes, 50 minutes, or 10 minutes. These averages can be applied to a chart using whatever number of bars (days) you find to be best for your trading style and risk tolerance. The key here is to find what is most meaningful to you.

Legends, Language, and Lore of Traders

When it comes to traders, one of the true legends is W. D. Gann, a stock and commodity trader who was also a prolific writer. His theories on time and price market activity are still used—and debated. Among his storied accomplishments was a forecast—published in 1928—that predicted the 1929 U.S. stock market high and the crash that followed.

Here's an example that Jim Sebanc gives for understanding why moving averages work. Let's say you want to buy a house that has been on the market for $200,000 for roughly nine months. And let's say your down payment that you've saved together with your borrowing power equal $200,000. But when you are ready to buy that house for $200,000, the price has risen to $225,000. Your first reaction may be that you're not going to pay $225,000 because you think it's worth only $200,000. In moving-average terminology, your "moving average" is $200,000; the market price is $225,000.

A few months later the price of the house is up to $235,000. And now you're starting to think that maybe this house *is* worth more than $200,000. Time and price have changed your perception. Your moving average is now moving up, but still lags the market. Then, a couple of months later, the price of the house goes up to $250,000. Now you think that you should have bought the house at $225,000. This means that your perception of value (your moving average) went from $200,000 to $225,000 over this period of time, as the selling price went to up $250,000. Your perception of price (moving average) is still lagging the market, but is above your original $200,000 level. If your moving average is representative of the rest of the potential buyers for this house, it would sell immediately at $225,000 because the price has come down to what is now perceived as fair value—changed by the movement of price over time.

This simple example illustrates why moving averages work. They show the average of prices for a given period of time up to the present, compared to the current value of whatever market or item you're tracking. Remember, the goal of using moving averages is to help you decide when to buy or sell by identifying the trend and relative momentum of the market, given your time frame, trading strategy, and risk tolerance.

As we study moving averages, as well as the other indicators addressed in the chapter, we're going to use the same process we did with the price-only chart. Each time you add an indicator to a chart, look at the chart with just that one indicator, in this case a moving average. As we begin, apply a moving average—any time frame that you choose—to a price-only chart. Don't have any expectations about what you will or should see. Just look. Now ask yourself, what is the correlation between the moving average and the price? What happens when the market price touches or crosses the moving average line? Do you see something meaningful? How reactive does the moving average line appear to be? Do the tops and bottoms of the moving average lag or correlate closely with the tops and bottoms of the market? Notice the change in the relative slope of the market versus the moving average. When the market price touches or crosses the moving average, does it accelerate, reverse, or stop?

Keep in mind that moving averages of various time frames will tell you different things. In general, moving averages of a longer time frame will lag the market because they take into account a greater amount of time. In addition, they tend to smooth the overall trend. Moving averages of shorter time frames will track the market more closely and therefore tend to be more reactive. There is no right or wrong moving average to use. Rather, you must decide which moving average is the most useful for your style of trading. For example, if you were trading with a long-term perspective (a buy-and-hold type of strategy) it would make sense to use longer-term moving averages such as the 50-, 100-, and/or 200-day moving averages (see Figure 3.2). For shorter-term trades, you'd use shorter time frames, as well as intraday averages for day trades and to help you decide entry and exit points (see Figure 3.3).

But at this point, our purpose is only to become familiar with moving averages, and the relationship between these averages and the market. **This process is one of the keys to understanding the dynamics of price behavior.**

It may be helpful to look at the screen without the market prices. (Most charting software will allow you to display just the moving averages and not the prices.) As you look at the moving average line, what significant features stand out, such as peaks and valleys, widening or contracting? Mark those junctures on the moving average lines. Now, replace the price data. How did the significant points along the moving averages correlate with the price movement? For example, did a peak on a moving average line closely precede or lag a top in the market? (Depending on the pattern, they

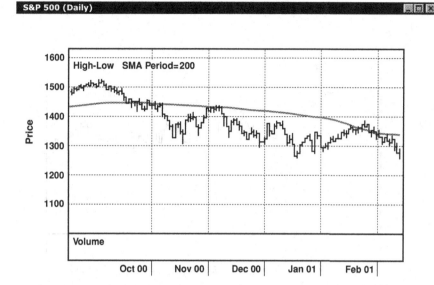

Figure 3.2   S&P 500 I (Daily) (*Source:* www.dtnfs.com, DTN Financial Services)

can even precede the top even though they are a lagging indicator.) Or was the moving average too slow to accurately predict a change in market trend?

At this point, has this exercise changed your perception or understanding from the price-only chart that you studied? Do you have a better feel for the dynamics? Or has it confused you? If the latter, change the length of the moving average, making it shorter or longer; then examine how this new moving average line correlates with the market. Does this new line more closely correlate with the original buy and sell points that you identified on the price-only chart?

Keep in mind that your ultimate goal is to find a moving average that will confirm or improve the signals for the price points (the buys and sells) that you previously identified on the price-only charts. Once you have achieved that, you will have a confirmation tool—

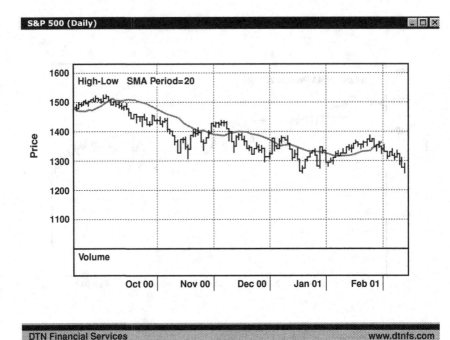

Figure 3.3 S&P 500 I (Daily) (*Source:* www.dtnfs.com, DTN Financial Services)

meaning a tool that you can use to confirm the buy and sell signals that you identify.

Repeat this same process as you study a second moving average, then a third, a fourth, and so on. Each time, just look at the chart with no expectations. What do you see in this moving average? Add the prices. What is the correlation between this moving average and the price? Now, examine the new moving average (see Figure 3.4) in the context of the previous one. What is the correlation between the moving averages, and how do they both correlate to the market?

Each time you add a moving average line, examine first its correlation to the market. Then add the previous moving averages, and view the correlation between the averages. For example, in Figure 3.4 you can see the 50-day and 200-day moving averages correlate near the peak of the market, but then quickly diverge.

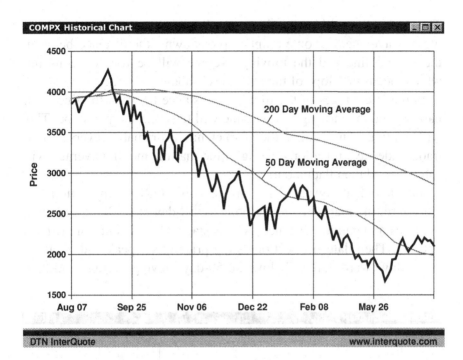

Figure 3.4 SCOMPX Historical Chart (*Source:* www.interquote.com, DTN Financial Services)

Many technicians apply numerous moving averages to their charts. Jim Sebanc uses 20 per time frame, displayed 10 each on two different charts. To the untrained eye, these scrawling lines on his screens look like platefuls of spaghetti. But to Jim, each of the moving averages tells a different story of momentum, trend, and volatility.

More than just the rising and falling of the moving average line and the market, there are other interpretations that can be applied to moving averages. Among them is the distance or gap between the moving average line and the market and the relative slopes of the two lines.

In an uptrend, the market will be considerably above a longer-term moving average. In a downtrend, it will be considerably below the longer-term moving average.

Keep in mind that in the early stages of a trend, the distance between the market and a longer-term moving average will increase.

The market line will have a sharper incline or slope compared with the moving average. At some point—up or down—the distance between the market line and the moving average will be roughly constant, which means the slope of the two lines is about the same.

In the later stages of the trend, the distance between the lines will narrow, and the moving average line will have the sharper slope. This will continue until either the market has a dramatic reversal or it trades sideways for a long enough time that the moving average will catch up and then flatten out.

Take a look at Figure 3.5 for Oracle Corp. (ORCL). In Section 1 of the figure, the market is above both the 50-day and 200-day moving averages and gaining distance. At this stage, ORCL is in a short-term uptrend. Then, later in Section 1, the price hits a peak and begins a move downward, falling below the 50-day moving average and then

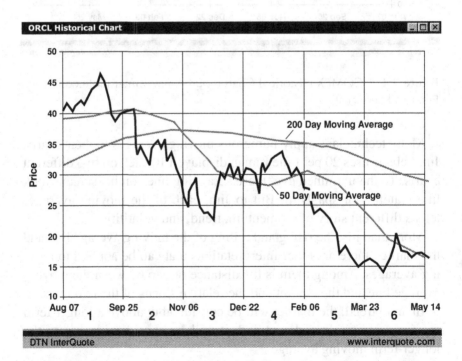

Figure 3.5 ORCL Historical Chart (*Source:* www.interquote.com, DTN Financial Services)

the 200-day moving average. ORCL at this point was in a downtrend. In Section 3, ORCL trades to a low and then trades steadily higher. It crosses and recrosses the 50-day line, and then in Section 4 the stock nears the 200-day line but cannot get above it. The stock then declines rapidly, breaking through the 50-day line. At Section 5, the price line is at the widest gap versus the moving average. This is often indicative of significant highs or significant lows.

As mentioned previously, one of the characteristics to observe is the distance between the market price and the moving average (such as at the lows in Sections 3 and 5 of the Oracle chart). For example, in an uptrend the farther the market is above any moving average, the less likely it is to break below it on the first attempt. And should it break below that line, it probably won't go very far below—nor for very long. The market's tendency will be to bounce back over the line.

Similarly, in a downtrend, the farther the market is below the moving average, the less likely it will rally above the moving average. And if it were to rally, the less likely it is that it would go very far above the line or trade above it for very long.

Why? Because it would take a lot of energy for the market to hit a faraway target and go through it. The exception would be if there were some major surprise to propel it in one direction or another—such as we saw when Iraq invaded Kuwait or Russia defaulted on its debt in July 1998.

This kind of distance/energy analysis can be applied to any moving average.

Figure 3.6 is the same six-month price chart for ORCL, but now with a 10-day moving average. The distance between the two lines narrows and widens, narrows and widens, frequently. And since the average is based on a relatively short time period, the 10-day moving average has less time lag vis-à-vis the market, and it is not as smooth as the longer-term 50-day or 200-day moving average.

We each have our own ways of explaining how we sense and gauge a change in market direction or sentiment, when an up move is running out of gas, or when we're nearing a bottom and we're likely to see a turnaround. Returning to our ocean-wave analogy, you can feel, hear, and see the difference in the tide. In the same way, you can begin

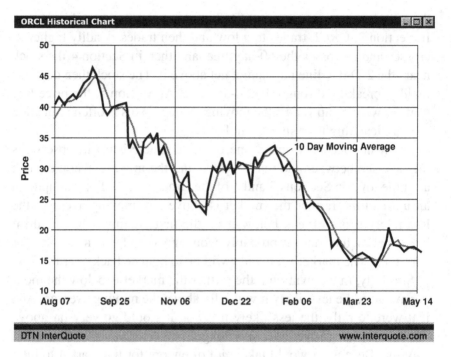

Figure 3.6 ORCL Historical Chart (*Source:* www.interquote.com, DTN Financial Services)

to see the changes in the market as you study the charts and indicators. And, as you get in sync with the market, you'll be able to sense the change in sentiment.

Another way to look at moving averages is within a certain distance—or envelope—above and below the moving average. For example, you may want to view the market activity within an envelope defined as a certain percentage above and below the moving average. Once again, you will have to do your own testing to pick the most effective percentage for your time frame, your trading style, and the market (stock or index) that you're trading. Jim, for example, looks at a variety of envelopes, ranging from very narrow to very wide.

First, take your favorite moving average, the one that you've found to be the most useful for your trading style, time frame, and risk tolerance. Then, you plot a certain percentage envelope above

---

Legends, Language, and Lore of Traders

"Floor order flow" is a concept that's hard to convey to a screen trader, but it's something I honed in the trading pit over the years. As you stand in the pit surrounded by a screaming, shouting, and sweating mass, you can detect subtle shifts in sentiment. It's a combination of factors, from how aggressive the buyers or the sellers are to how quickly the bids and offers are snapped up. Then there are more subjective measures, like the body language of the brokers who are filling customer orders. Do they seem rushed and frazzled, like they have a lot of orders to execute quickly, or are they more casual in their demeanor and seem to be waiting for their prices?

When there is a noticeable change in that sentiment, a local trader like myself—who is strictly day trading—will adjust accordingly. There have been days when I have had a bullish opinion all the way from the office, where I've conferred with our technicians and fellow traders, to the Chicago Mercantile Exchange a couple of blocks away. Then, once I step onto the floor, the mood of the pit is decisively different. The opening bell sounds and the sellers step up aggressively and, if I've been on my toes, I'm right there with them—even though the bearish sentiment is contrary to my own original opinion. A little later the market may test a support level and begin to rally; then the bullish opinion I held earlier will take over, and I'll trade from the long side.

In trading, it's not what you think or believe. Yes, you'll form opinions based on your technical analysis. But in the end, it's the market's own behavior and *how fast you adapt to it* that will determine how you should trade. If you don't adapt you lose.

---

and below the moving average. That defines a band of possible price activity that is X percent above and X percent below the moving average. Now, scroll backward in time on the price chart. How often does the stock, index, or futures contract trade or stop at that upper or lower envelope? The goal of this exercise is to find at what percentage—above or below the moving average—the market tends to stop. In a volatile market the percentage will be larger, and in a more stable market the percentage will be smaller. Also, the length of time spanned by the moving average (i.e., the periods) will help determine what percent is more appropriate. For example, 1 percent above and below a 200-day moving average would mean very little since it is a very small percentage applied to a comparatively long-term indicator. However, a 0.5 percent envelope above and below a five-bar moving average (measuring the moving average of the previous five bars on the chart) may be very important. While the percentage is small, the envelope may be meaningful because it is based on an ultra-short-term moving average.

Reconfiguring your chart for a 5 percent envelope, see how often the stock or futures contract that you're studying has been within this 5 percent envelope. What happened in the past when it touched the upper reaches of this 5 percent envelope? Did it break through to the upside, or did it quickly reverse? What are the typical percentage moves that this market makes in correlation to the time frame and moving average that you are using? Studying this recent price pattern will give you hints for the kind of moves you could expect—all things being equal—in the near term.

For example, if a stock has not traded outside a 5 percent envelope versus its 50-day moving average for the past several months, you could expect that a 5 percent envelope would contain any breakouts or breakdowns in the near future—especially the *farther* the market had to go to hit the envelope and the *shorter* the period of time in which to do so. In other words, if the S&Ps had to move 80 points in one day, it's going to be much tougher to get through the defined envelope than if the market only had to go 2 points in a day or 80 points in a week. For example, let's say the market is 80 points below the envelope. If it goes those 80 points quickly, it will be less likely to get through any significant line or envelope there. Why? Because the market probably has expended a lot of energy to go those 80 points and may be running out of gas (or momentum). However, if the market trends upward 75 points over a week or two and now is only 5 points from the envelope, the next move could easily surpass it.

There are other kinds of envelopes that can be applied to moving averages, namely those based on standard deviation, as well as equi-linear, average change, mean deviation, Bollinger bands, and Keltner channels, among others.

For our purposes, we have discussed percentage-based envelopes that show extreme moves. Others that we use are standard deviation envelopes that can give good insight into market congestion and probable breakouts, along with extension targets.

At this point, your study of technical analysis has just begun. Most importantly, you've focused on the price chart to determine what it can tell you. Any chart is meaningful, whether it shows the last five ticks, five days, five months, or five years. The key is to train your eye to discover chart formations and the small formations (or fractyls) within the bigger formations. If at any point along the way you become lost or confused, simply turn back to this chapter and start at the beginning. It's all in the chart, and if you become a dedicated student of this discipline, you may see the message within.

4

Technical Analysis 102

"The trend is your friend," the old trading adage goes. But what, exactly, is the prevailing trend? In this chapter we will address trend lines and what they illustrate in the market. A trend line is a linear, graphical representation of at least two points in the market that attempt to identify the general trend, or the trend of the extreme limits. Those points could be from one significant low to another, between two highs, or between a low and a high. Conceivably, you could use any two points on a chart (since every price on a chart is part of the market). But the most telling trend lines are usually those drawn between two significant, consecutive highs and two significant, consecutive lows.

TREND LINES

As you'll recall in Chapter 3, when you look at a price chart certain patterns and features stand out, such as the peaks (highs) and valleys (lows). Trend lines then can be drawn on the chart, connecting those highs or lows, and extended out into the future. The trend line projects a path that the market would take if it continued on its course. Remember, Newtonian physics states that an object in motion will continue that motion until it meets an equal or opposite force. The same thing applies to the market. A stock or index that is trending in one direction will tend to continue that trend until it meets with an equal or opposite force in the form of support or resistance—and very often this change can be very abrupt.

Thus, as the market moves up and down in smaller gyrations within an overall pattern, the trend lines identify the potential areas of significant force—meaning where it's likely to hit resistance to slow or stop an uptrend or to find support to slow or stop a downtrend.

To begin, take a chart of any stock or index, since these methods apply to all markets that trade. Figure 4.1 is a chart of the Dow Jones Industrial Average (symbol INDU).

Just looking at the chart, two of the features that stand out are the peak in early March and then the next peak in late March. The line

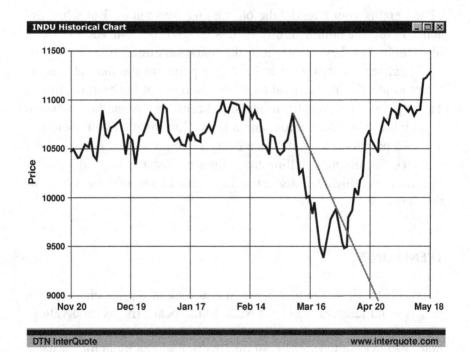

Figure 4.1 INDU Historical Chart (*Source:* www.interquote.com, DTN Financial Services)

drawn between these two consecutive highs forms a trend line that marks resistance that this market faces on the upside. Then later in April, once the market was able to get above that trend line, it rallied steadily.

Similarly, let's look at a trend line formed by two significant lows. Figure 4.2 is a chart of the Nasdaq Composite.

Draw a line from the low in late July to the low made in mid-October, and then extend that line into the future. This line shows the support level under the market from mid-October through December. (Looking farther into the future, the market traded above this line in January and February, and then touched it in early March before trading higher.)

Other trend lines extend from a significant high to a significant low, or from a significant low to a significant high. These types of trend

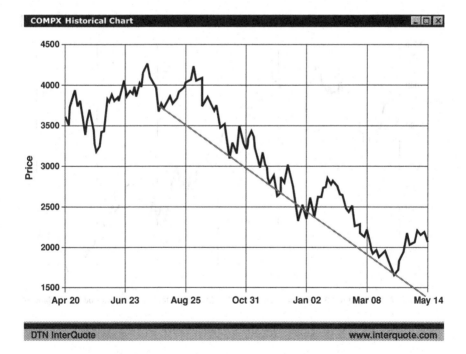

Figure 4.2 COMPX Historical Chart (Nasdaq Composite Index—Combine) (*Source:* www.interquote.com, DTN Financial Services)

lines are the most useful when each point is part of a separate, but consecutive chart pattern. For example, you might start the line at a significant high point at the end of an uptrend, and then select a low in a rangebound pattern that follows.

Figure 4.3 is an example of such a trend line, using the same Nasdaq chart as in Figure 4.2. This type of high to low (or low to high) trend line can be drawn in several places. One example is from the mid-July high, which is at the end of an uptrend pattern, to the mid-October low, which is part of a sharp sell-off pattern. This trend line, when extended into the future, is support when the market is above this line and resistance when it trades below it. Going forward, lines like this are significant, especially as the market approaches them. For example, if the market were trading below this type of trend line, one

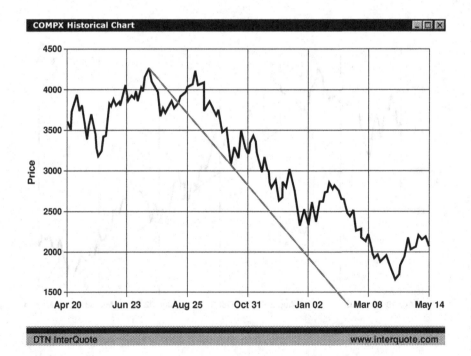

Figure 4.3 COMPX Historical Chart (*Source:* www.interquote.com, DTN Financial Services)

would look for the market to face considerable resistance as it approached the line.

As with moving averages, discussed in Chapter 3, a variety of trend lines can be drawn and applied to the same chart. But just as we did in our exercises in Chapter 3, it's important not to rush the steps. Rather, take each trend line you apply to a chart one at a time. What does it show you? When the line is extended, what significant highs and/or lows does it touch?

Applying different trend lines to your chart—and studying each, one at a time—you may find that some are more meaningful to you than others. For example, a trend line that touches one or more highs (or lows) shows an area of resistance (or support).

Additionally, there are other kinds of lines that can be applied to a chart. One type is the regression line that marks the mean of the market activity—the level around which much of the market activity has been centered. To draw a regression line, first choose a particular pattern on your chart. Now, draw a line that is in the middle of that price activity. (See Figure 4.4.) This line, which you've drawn by eye, can be made more exact by charting software that allows for regression lines to be drawn.

The resulting regression line bisects the market activity. Now, add two parallel lines—one above and one below—that connect two highs and two lows.

These three lines show you the median of the market (the regression line in the center) and the outer limits of this particular move. These parallel lines also form trend channels, which we will also discuss. In a trending market, you'd expect the activity to center around the regression line, with most up moves and down moves contained by the channel lines.

Trend channels can also be applied to any clearly defined trend. The top line is drawn between two or more highs. The bottom line is drawn between two or more lows. Figure 4.5 is an example of a trend channel drawn on a chart of Cisco Systems.

The bottom channel line connects three lows. The top channel line also connects three points. Interestingly, in Figure 4.5, the stock trades off when it breaks below the bottom line of the channel.

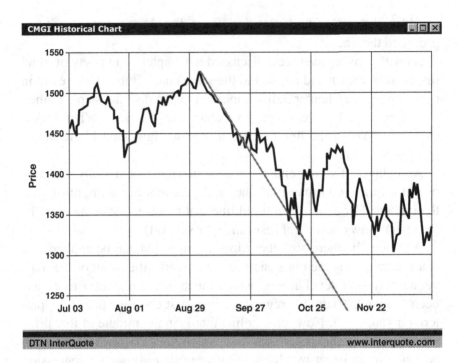

Figure 4.4 CMGI Historical Chart (*Source:* www.interquote.com, DTN Financial Services)

Channel lines can also be used to define trading ranges. In this case, the lines will be roughly horizontal, connecting high points above and low points below. When the market is in a trading range it is in a kind of holding pattern that is defined by no significant higher highs or significant lower lows. Rather, the market trades within those parameters. This might happen after the market has made a large move to the upside or the downside and is now consolidating. We sometimes refer to that as the market "taking a breath." In other words, buyers and sellers are active within a certain range, but there is no real impetus—at least at that point—to propel the market upward or downward.

But nothing stays in a range forever. As a trader, you'll be using your technical analysis to look for signs that the market is likely to test the outer limits of that trading range, either on the upside or on the downside. In Figure 4.6, McDonald's Corporation's stock traded in a

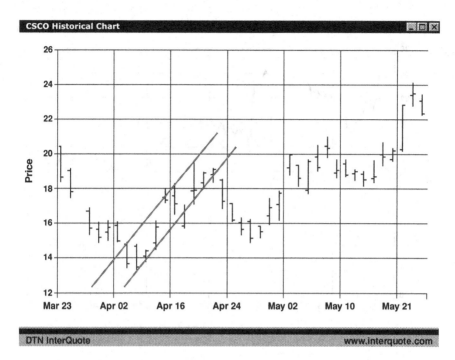

Figure 4.5   CSCO Historical Chart (Cisco Systems) (*Source:* www.interquote.com, DTN Financial Services)

range between roughly $29 and $31 a share from late January through late February 2001, when it broke below the bottom of the range and then traded significantly lower.

As you can see by these examples, the trend lines delineate support or resistance in the future, based on previous highs and lows.

Often, we think of a trading range as a sign of a dull or otherwise uneventful market. However, there are times when the market is in a trading range and resting for a big move to come. Usually, the longer the market stays in a trading range, the more potential it has to make a large move—up or down—once that range is exceeded. The exception to this is when the market is "dead," meaning it has little activity.

The chart patterns you identify tell a story of what is happening in the market at that time, reflecting the interplay between buyers and sellers. For example, in an uptrend the buyers are aggressive, eager to

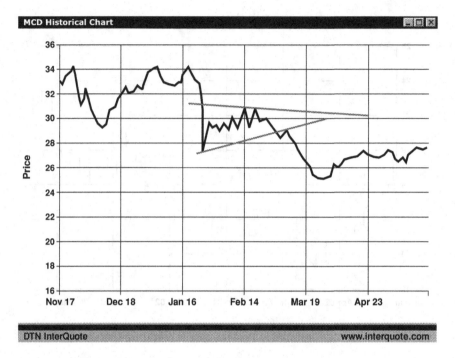

Figure 4.6   MCD Historical Chart (McDonald's Corporation) (*Source:* www.interquote.com, DTN Financial Services)

establish positions in a particular stock or index at whatever price the sellers are willing to give them.

In a downtrend, the opposite occurs. The sellers are more aggressive as they take profits on previous long positions, or as they establish short positions in anticipation that a particular stock or index is going down. In between, when the market is more or less in a sideways or rangebound pattern, there is a transition phase in which both sides participate. In this phase, buyers may be lightly establishing positions in anticipation of an up move, and sellers may be getting out of long positions or establishing small short positions in anticipation of a decline. Remember, what makes a market is not only the presence of buyers and sellers, but the confluence of opinions.

The strength or conviction of the prevailing market opinion can be seen in a bar chart that depicts buy and sell volume. Some software shows a volume chart for a stock. You'll see bars that are shaded one color for price lower (depicting sell volume is higher) and another for price higher (when buy volume is higher). These bars also show the volume for the time frame measured. Intraday or for the longer term, you can use the volume chart to help you see the bias or strength of conviction among the buyers and sellers in the market.

Before going on to the next set of indicators—oscillators—let's address the other kind of chart patterns that, with time and experience, may become meaningful to you. These patterns can be found on any chart, from very short-term measuring minutes to very long-term (several years). The patterns tell the same story, although the time frame to which the story applies differs.

BREAKOUTS AND TRIANGLES

When you look at a chart, it's fairly easy to see where the market has been. The challenge, obviously, is to determine where it's likely to go next. One of the things that traders look for is a sign of a pending breakout from an existing range. One potential breakout pattern to look for is the triangle or pennant formation.

Think of an isosceles triangle turned on its side with the apex or point facing to the right. This pattern is formed as the range of the market narrows. This contraction is caused by up and down movements that neither surpass previous highs nor go below previous lows. This kind of action has the effect of coiling a spring tighter and tighter until it propels itself outward. Similarly, when the market does break out of this tightening range, it is usually with increased volatility and volume and mostly in one direction for a period of time without a significant pullback.

As the market contracts, it becomes easier to see the triangle if you add trend lines, one connecting all the tops and one connecting all the bottoms. Extending those two lines (the top line sloping downward and the bottom line sloping upward), they will cross at some point in the future. That point becomes the apex of the triangle. The normal breakout point from this kind of pattern is often around three-quarters of the way from the base (beginning) of the triangle to where the apex would be.

After the breakout, moving averages will come into play as the market moves to the upside or downside. In this instance, the moving average (as discussed in Chapter 3) will help to confirm the trend that's taking place.

U's AND V's

Another pattern that traders look for in the market is a setup for a reversal. As the name implies, a reversal is a change in market direction—from uptrend to downtrend, or vice versa. This pattern of activity is marked by a V or U formation, depending on how dramatic the move turns out to be. For example, Figure 4.7 of Veritas (VRTS) shows a U formation at the low in early April and then again in the late April low before the early May move higher.

By comparison, in Figure 4.8 of BEA Systems (BEAS) a sharper V bottom is formed in early April.

In a very volatile market such as the Nasdaq, it's not uncommon for a trend to accelerate and then suddenly reverse. These trend/spike reversals occur not only at major tops and bottoms, but also along the way.

The challenge, however, is that these kinds of moves can catch even an experienced trader off guard. For example, say a market has been trending slowly higher for a month and then explodes to the upside for a few days. On the last day of the up move, it reverses suddenly and closes near its low of the day. That results in a spike high and a close near the low of the day, or at least in the lower third of the range for the day.

What happened in the market to cause this kind of spike reversal? Perhaps there was news that caused an upward movement, triggering buy stops. (Or negative news could cause a sharp downward move, triggering sell stops to accelerate the action.) If there is no follow-through, then the market will reverse—a sell-off following a spike reversal high or a rally following a spike reversal low.

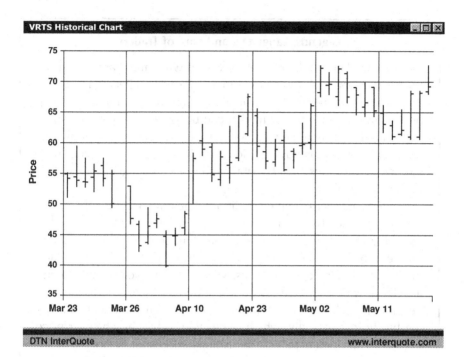

Figure 4.7 VRTS Historical Chart (Veritas) (*Source:* www.interquote.com, DTN Financial Services)

This kind of spike reversal—in either direction—reflects the "fourth C" in the Four Cs of trading.

1. Complacency—You feel you have nothing to worry about; the market is going your way, or at least it's not going against you.

2. Caution—The market makes a small move against you.

3. Concern—The market continues to move against you, and you start to feel rarely exercised muscles tighten uncomfortably.

4. Capitulation—You reach the "puke point" (see box) and you just can't take it anymore. You panic out of the position at any price.

Legends, Language, and Lore of Traders

As everyone knows, the market moves up when there are more buyers than sellers, and down when there are more sellers than buyers. But there are extremes. When it seems everyone is selling, pushing prices lower and lower, the market can become "oversold," meaning prices are lower than the technical and fundamental conditions warrant. Or, everyone is buying, bidding prices higher and higher until the market becomes "overbought," and prices are higher than conditions would warrant.

There is another extreme condition, thankfully lasting only a short amount of time. That is the "puke point." As the market moves dramatically in one direction or another, someone inevitably is caught on the wrong side. Perhaps you're long from the top of a move, and the market is being offered aggressively lower and you, unable to find a seller at your price, are forced to get out at any price. Or you may be short at the bottom and scrambling to cover in a market that is being bid up dramatically, which forces you to buy at whatever price you can. This point of panic—of rushing for the door before the building collapses—is known in trader terminology as the "puke point."

This may be a reference to the digestive disruption experienced by traders who are dealing with mounting losses. Or it may refer to the point at which the market itself dispels the buyers who had hung on for most of the break or the sellers who endured the worst of the rally. Whatever the origin, the puke point is not pleasantly endured when you're on the wrong side of the market.

M's AND W's

Looking at the charts, you can see that there are other patterns that are helpful in analyzing current market activity and determining what might happen next. Among them is the M or double top. (See Figure 4.8.) As the name implies, this formation resembles the double peak of a capital M after the market makes a high, sells off, makes a second high at or near the first level, and then fails again. This is known as a failed retest of the highs. Depending on other market dynamics, an

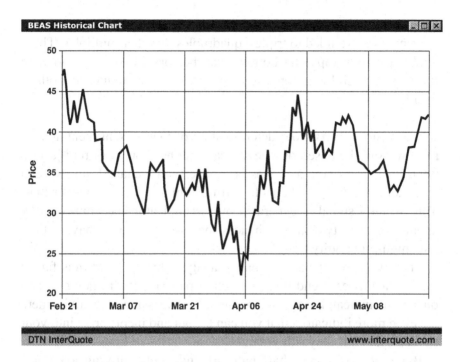

Figure 4.8 BEAS Historical Chart (BEA Systems Inc.) (*Source:* www.interquote.com, DTN Financial Services)

M top would add to the downward pressure and also reinforce the resistance at the highs. In Figure 4.8 an M is formed when the stock price (BEAS) trades to about $45, then breaks to about $37, before rallying to about $43, and then selling off again. Since the second high (43) is below the first (45) it is a classic M formation.

A W or double bottom is the opposite of the M top. The W is formed with a break, a bounce to a higher level, and then another break down to or near the first low level. Failing to penetrate that low level, the market bounces higher. This is a failed retest of the lows, which adds to the upside momentum from that level and reinforces support at the lows.

Another characteristic of the double top or bottom is that the retest (the second peak or valley) is formed with less volume than the first. In fact, the second top (or bottom) may not have the same extension as the first, but it is still a retest of that move. Further, double tops or bottoms may be extended to triples, quadruples, or other multiples. These double or triple tops and bottoms can be formed over a short time frame or a much longer one, some occurring over minutes and others over decades.

In technical analysis, your determination of market sentiment and direction won't be based on one indicator alone. You can't rely just on trend lines or moving averages or a pattern on a chart. Using several indicators concurrently helps to form a confluence of signals or bias. Thus when a signal is generated by one indicator and confirmed by another or even two more, chances increase that you'll have a low-risk, high-probability trade.

This overview of basic technical analysis has focused thus far on moving averages, trend lines, and chart patterns. We're going to add one more indicator—oscillators—to the discussion. Certainly there are even more indicators that you can try out and incorporate into your trading system if they suit your needs.

But if you observe chart patterns and apply moving averages, trend lines, and oscillators to your charts, you may find that you have a strong base on which to evaluate the market and build your trading system.

OSCILLATORS

An oscillator measures the progression/momentum of the fluctuations in the price of a stock or index. When a market is volatile—making dramatic moves—the oscillator applied to a chart will have dramatic rises and falls resembling a shock wave. When a market is calm, the oscillator will have small fluctuations resembling the heartbeat of a patient at rest.

Stochastics are a technical indicator that compares a stock's closing price to its price range over a period of time. The premise is that when a stock is rising it tends to close near the high, while a stock that is falling tends to close near its low. (There are many books and web sites that discuss and use various kinds of stochastics in depth.) For our purpose, we will use one kind of stochastic known as the "slow stochastic." Most charting software programs will allow you to pick from a menu of indicators, including the slow stochastic. Check the default setting. You will need to adjust this setting to pick various input parameters, including your time frame, such as 20-bar (or 20-day), 13-bar (or 13-day), or 8-bar (8-day). As with the moving average, you are looking for the time frame that best suits your trading input parameters and that tends to confirm your trading signals.

As you study stochastics or any other indicator the process begins the same way. Pull up a chart of any stock or index with no other lines or indicators on it. Now, apply a slow stochastic to your chart, choosing a parameters (such as 8, 13, or 20 bars or days). How does this line correlate with the prices you see on your chart? Does the stochastic line rise or fall in tandem with the market, or is it too fast or too slow? Now adjust the input and parameters of the stochastic and see how it correlates with the market activity.

Your goal is to find a parameter of the stochastic that you can use *in conjunction with* your other indicators. For example, you may find that the 20-bar slow stochastic tracks the market closely. Further, you may see that the stochastic closely correlates with the peak of a trend, just before a sharp break occurs.

What happens when you apply the trend lines and moving averages that you've previously identified? Does the oscillator intersect the top of the rally near or at the resistance trend line that you identified? How does the oscillator tend to confirm the moving average?

Look at the chart of the S&P futures (Figure 4.9). A trend line drawn between previous highs pinpoints the top of the move at 1407. A second trend line drawn between previous lows intersects the market at 1395. With the market below that first trend line, we have an initial sell signal.

Now, we apply our moving average, which peaks at 1387 and then declines as the market sells off. Third, we add a 20-day slow stochastic, which lags the other two indicators but confirms the sell a day later at 1371.

How would you use that information? Depending on your time

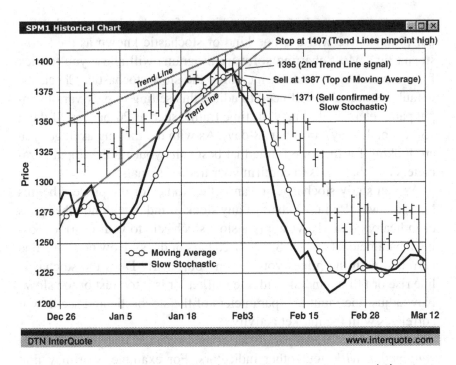

Figure 4.9   S&P Futures with Trend Lines, Moving Average, and Slow Stochastic

frame and your experience level, you might have gone short at 1395 based on the trend lines for a day trade, or you may have watched for the confirmation from the second indicator when the moving average turned down at 1387. Or because of having two sell signals already, you might assume the stochastic to so indicate—which it does at 1371.

Keep in mind that there is no hard-and-fast formula. It's not the sum of trend line "X," moving average "Y," and oscillator "Z," divided by the time frame you're looking at. This kind of technical analysis is more like navigation. The map you use is the price chart. The indicators are like the coordinates that you mark to plot the course of your ship from point A to point B. You may run into rough seas or a headwind en route that could slow you down, or a storm could blow you off course. But the coordinates help you to plot your direction. In the same way, the indicators you use—looking at various time frames to find the one that matches your trading parameters—will help you to plot your strategy of going long or short and at what price level.

Further, the trend line on your chart can help you plot your trailing stops. A trailing stop is one that moves in the direction of your trade. For example, if you buy stock X at 20 with a stop at 19 and targets of 22 and 24, as the price moves higher you could raise the level of the stop. You can move the trailing stop upward or downward in the same direction as the market movement, keeping it just outside your trend line. So if you go short S&P futures at 1395, you may decide to place your stop just outside the trend line at 1407. (See Figure 4.9.) When the market goes down, you may move that stop along the trend line to 1395, and then 1392, 1388, and so forth—depending on the duration of your trade and your risk tolerance.

Using three indicators—trend lines, moving averages, and oscillators—you have three "opinions" on the tone and direction of the market. They may not be in agreement at the same time or the same price level. Some signals will be early and some will be late. But when you have a consensus among your indicators, you have a confirmation that may result in a low-risk, high-probability trade.

After all, that is the goal of trading. You want to use indicators to move the odds in your favor and limit your risk. It's trial and error as you experiment with the kinds of indicators and time frames that you apply. With diligent study, however, you will find the indicators that suit your trading the best.

WATCHING THE INDEXES

Stock traders reading this book may wonder why most of the examples reflect the stock index futures. Yes, these indexes do represent the broader equities market. But there is another valuable reason. Stock indexes, themselves, are a leading indicator for many stocks. In other words, what's happening in an index gives a glimpse of what might be happening soon in a particular stock, and vice versa.

This may be most evident in those stocks that dominate a particular index. In the S&P 500, for example, stocks such as Microsoft have large weightings. Thus, if S&P futures are trading off their highs, you could expect that Microsoft will soon follow suit. Conversely, if the S&Ps are rallying into the close, Microsoft is likely—barring a company-specific news announcement—also to settle strongly.

The correlation of the indexes—Nasdaq, S&P, and Dow—with major stocks in these indexes can be a valuable indicator for individual equity traders. As a stock trader, what you're looking for is the strength (or weakness) of a particular stock compared with the index. If a major Nasdaq stock such as Oracle is rallying, you know it will have a positive impact on the Nasdaq. Or, if the Nasdaq is breaking but Oracle is still up on the day, there's a good chance that Oracle will soon be under pressure.

Even if you trade individual equities exclusively, you need to keep a close eye on the indexes to give you an indication of what's going on in the broader market and to help confirm the bullish and/or bearish signals that your stock-specific indicators are generating. Put another way, the sentiment of the indexes reflects the sentiment of the market. During surprise moves, the futures market may move first and therefore presage a potential move in the individual stocks. During quieter times in the market, the individual stocks tend to move before the futures, and in this instance the stocks would be the advance indicators. The analysis of both is important, and both should be watched carefully for confirmation or contradiction.

5

The Myths, the Risks, and the Rewards

By now, you're ready to begin trading. Or perhaps you're already dabbling in the market. This is when the mental game becomes crucial. This is the point when the demons of greed and fear will rear their ugly heads. This is the point at which you could fall prey to some of the dangers that will undermine your trading.

THE MYTH YOU MUST FORGET

Every day trader has been told at one time in his or her career, "If you make $500 a day, or $2,500 a week, then at the end of the year—taking into account two weeks off for vacation—you'll have made $125,000 a year." That is the single worst piece of advice a day trader could ever get. Why? Because no two trading days are the same.

For instance, if you as a day trader did not aggressively participate in the market—trading in and out all day, every day—from October 2000 to April 2001, then you missed what was arguably one of the greatest periods for day trading that the market has every seen. For example, on April 4, 2001, the Nasdaq experienced a hard break. Nasdaq futures opened at 1406, traded to a high of 1450, and then broke to a low of 1360, settling at 1379.50. How can that compare with a quiet, narrow-range trading day that you might see during the summer lull?

There is another misconception that must also be avoided when you're day trading: the belief that you can "average" $500 a day. The problem is that it leads to the thinking that if you lose $500 in one day, to keep up with the average the next day you need to make $1,000. This kind of thinking is a gross misunderstanding of how to get capital, maintain capital, and become a profitable trader.

Rather, your goal as a day trader should be that you will have your best days when the market is the most volatile. If this is not the case, you need to reexamine your trading methods. One thing that is difficult to understand is why people want to stop trading when they're making money. The thinking along those lines is, "Oh, I made X dollars today. That's it. I'm done." Why not say to yourself, "I'm really hot today. If this market is volatile enough, I'll stay here and make some more money." This is the old "strike while the iron is hot" mentality. When the market is "cold," there is no volatility to speak of, and it's a lackluster trade, then you can comfortably sit on the sidelines or treat yourself to a day at the golf course or the beach!

One note of caution: Know when, mentally and physically, you're done. If you have a profitable day and you feel in sync with the market, it's a good idea to keep trading—as long as your mental focus is there. But if you feel fatigued at all, you must be honest with yourself about when it's time to call it quits.

JUDGING VOLATILITY

How do you know when the market is volatile? The best way is to plot activity on a spreadsheet. Do not use your data feed or your chart feed for this. Rather, it's a much more hands-on learning experience if you create a spreadsheet into which you plug the numbers from the trading session. For example, at our trading firm my partner, Brad Sullivan, instructs the junior traders to input the hourly ranges from the Nasdaq and S&P futures into a spreadsheet. As a result, we know what the average range of trades for the first hour has been for any trading day in the past five years. Is that important? We think so.

LOSING SYNDROME

Another potential losing syndrome is the inability to leave when the market is going against you. As you know by now (or as you'll soon know), it's much easier to stop when you're up money than when you're down money. But from our experience and by observing others, every trader needs to have a personal "stop loss point" for a day session. Whatever your trading style, you must have a loss limit and the discipline to enforce it. But how do you determine what that loss level should be?

If your best day ever is making, say, $10,000, your personal stop point can't be at a $30,000 loss. Rather, it should be placed at a logical point for your trading, your capitalization, and your risk tolerance. Also, if you're a person who typically earns $100,000 a year trading, you do not want to risk 20 percent of that in one day.

There are various disciplinary approaches. For example, Brad tells of a friend of his who trades in the Eurodollar futures pit. He leaves the Eurodollar pit every day at 9:30 A.M. Central time after trading for two hours and 10 minutes. Win, lose, or draw, he leaves.

TRADING IS A JOB

Trading is so "cool." It's so "glamorous." There's a definite appeal to trading. But the truth, however, is that it's a job—a profession—that requires dedication and hard work.

One of the Chicago newspapers interviewed a day trader who was in her second year of trading after quitting her law career. In the interview, she said that one of the reasons she loves trading is that, rather than working 70 hours a week as a lawyer, she now works from 8:15 A.M. until 3:15 P.M.

From that comment, it appears this day trader has a slim chance of ever making $500,000 or of becoming an accomplished trader. The job of trading extends far beyond the market hours. You have to hone your skills, your craft. Trading is a profession that may take some time and involve some difficulty in getting to the point where you want to be. Granted, the market hours are abbreviated compared with a normal workday. But when you're trading, it can envelope your whole life. It's a 24/7 "profession/obsession." You will become consumed by the market and by the desire to learn more.

That's a sobering thought for many would-be traders who have left a career and are trying their hands at the market. But they must ask themselves, "How many people trade their own money and make $1 million or more a year?"

GOAL SETTING

As stated at the opening of the chapter, you can't set a daily profit target, multiply it by the number of trading days in the year, and then say, "Oh, I'm going to make $125,000 or $250,000 or whatever." The only daily financial mark you should have is the limit that you'd lose in one day before walking away.

Otherwise, you must be more forward thinking in your financial goals.

This requires a particular mental discipline. Obviously, you are cognizant of the financial side of your trading. Setting weekly and monthly goals is an acknowledgment of that. But by not having a daily goal, you disassociate *each trade* and *each tick* from the money that you'll make. Remember, your goal is to make well-executed trades instead of making "X" on each trade. Focusing on making good trades in the near term, while keeping a weekly financial goal, helps you to retain your discipline while maximizing the potential of making low-risk, high-probability trades.

When Brad and I began training traders, we saw goal setting as an important part of their development. We require each trader to have weekly, monthly, and quarterly goals—at three different levels. We begin with weekly goals:

1. The first level is a goal that is attainable for every week one trades.

2. The second level is a higher goal that is expected to be reached when the market is trading in a more volatile fashion. (The greater the volatility, the more opportunities there are to trade.)

3. The third-level goal is 15 times greater than the first-level goal. As Brad explains, that third-level goal is, understandably, a very difficult one to reach—one that he has reached only once in the past two years.

Traders then set goals along the same lines—with three levels of attainment—on a monthly basis.

(Brad's other goals for himself include never having a losing week—a goal he is still striving for. Another is to have his biggest winning week of the year be a minimum of 10 times greater than the biggest losing week.)

Focusing on weekly or monthly goals allows a trader to focus outward. Otherwise the temptation will be to focus on the next trade, the next tick, the afternoon session—which will undermine discipline and the ability to make well-executed trades each time.

After an incident such as a significant losing day that destabilizes a trader's confidence or trading rhythm, it's vitally important to keep that focus on the longer term. As you trade, you will be tempted to see the next trading session or even the next trade as the "one that will make it all back." Here's an example. Let's say your maximum allowed daily trading loss is $5,000, and you lose that in one day. The next day, you should not come in thinking, "I'm going to make $5,000 to get that money back." Rather, you should sit back and analyze what happened. Most likely, it was due to the loss of some type of psychological control.

Focusing beyond the next trading session, you can set a goal for yourself to make back that $5,000 in the next five days, nine days, or whatever time period makes sense for your trading style. This process doesn't change over time, not if you reach the ranks of traders who are trading significant size. If your maximum allowed daily loss is $100,000 and you reach it one day, you'll have the same mental process as the trader who has a maximum allowed loss of $1,000.

The process is always the same: Look forward and trade wisely and retain your stroke to get that money back.

ADJUSTING GOALS FOR SIZE

As you gain experience and increase your trade size, the goals you set for yourself, as a day trader, need to be adjusted. A trader increases trade size—without exposing too much capital on a percentage basis—because of an increase in profits. Now that trader must take a look at his or her trading statistics. Let's assume that this day trader averaged 35 ticks on winning trades in the S&P futures market and 18 ticks on the losing trades. Then, at this point, the trader doubles trade size, going from being a two-lot (two contracts at a time) trader to a four-lot trader. It might be that all of a sudden, with the increase in trade size, the statistics are negatively impacted. Now, the average winner is 13 ticks and the average loser is 22 ticks.

What happened? With the increase in trade size, the trader is now thinking about the money on the line with each trade. The only solution is to adjust the mental game. The skills this trader exhibited when trading two lots are the same skills that will allow for a potential doubling of income. The trade execution is there; the focus has to be on making good trades—and not on the money.

The same rules of trading apply whether you're a beginning trader or you've been at this 5, 10, or more years. Always, the focus is on two goals:

1. **Preservation of capital**

2. **Making well-executed trades**

If you can focus on these two objectives, you will go a long way to extending your trading life and your profit potential. In 20 years of trading, I can't tell you how many blowouts I've witnessed. It generally comes down to one of two scenarios:

Perhaps a trader has a promising beginning with several successful trades in a row. Trading seems to come naturally to him or her. He (or she) loosens up on the discipline, maybe trading without stops. What's really happened, however, is that this trader's style is exactly in sync with the market at the moment. He likes to buy dips and sell rallies, and he's in a rangebound market. It goes down, he buys. It goes up, he sells. Very smooth and (deceivingly) easy. Then the market breaks out of that range. He buys a dip, and the market falls sharply. Without a stop, he's got a huge loss and no one to buy what he's selling on the way down. Or, he sells a rally, but the market skyrockets. Again, without a stop, he's got a huge loss, and no one wants to sell so he can cover his short.

The other scenario is that of a trader who never seems to make much headway. Make a little . . . lose a little. . . . This can be very frustrating, although it's exactly what's expected when you're starting out. Then the trader makes a little more and loses a little more, and a little more still. Now he (or she) feels he's behind the eight ball. He trades a bigger position, hoping to make up for previous losses. Then he loses even more. Completely disheartened, the trader makes a suicidal, all-or-nothing trade. He lays it all on the line in one big trade that, if unsuccessful, will take him out of the market. This is the trader's death wish: a loss so big it will end all the pain. More often than not, he'll get that wish.

What these two scenarios show is the impact of unrealistic expectations when you're starting out. If you focus only on making money, you will severely undermine your ability to succeed.

Capital preservation and making well-executed trades should govern everything you do as a trader. When you deviate from one, you automatically violate the other. They transcend everything else in importance because they encompass everything else—from the mental preparation to technical analysis. If you take nothing else away from this book, keep these two rules somewhere handy when you trade:

1. **Preserving my capital allows me to come back to trade another day.**

2. **When I focus on well-executed trades—instead of making money—I have the best chance of succeeding.**

Now let's take these topics one at a time.

CAPITAL PRESERVATION

As outlined in Chapter 2, how you trade will be governed by how much money you have. In futures, the minimum account size is $5,000 to trade one S&P e-mini overnight or two intraday. In stocks, you can use leverage to increase your capital 2-to-1 or as much as 6-to-1 for day trading. Therefore—particularly in stocks—there is theoretically no such thing as an undercapitalized trader. If you have $100, you could conceivably trade a few shares of a $10 stock. We'll assume you have several thousand dollars—anywhere from $5,000 to $50,000—that you're willing to risk for the purposes of undertaking day trading. But regardless of the amount of money, you must view this as seed capital that should never be seriously depleted. Viewing it as that, you'll have the right respect for money that goes with trading.

The problem for many traders is that "capital preservation" sounds like something that would concern a conservative investor who buys only triple–A rated municipal bonds: nice and safe, but with a comparatively low return. What I'm suggesting here is to take that focus on capital preservation and apply it to trading, which is inherently one of the riskiest endeavors you could imagine. Sounds like a contradiction, doesn't it?

Yes . . . and no. This emphasis on capital preservation will allow you to keep your losses to a strict minimum, while letting your profits run. To do that, you must adhere to the 2-to-1 rule:

For every $1 that you lose per trade, you must make a minimum of $2 ($2.50 is even better) before commissions. Put the other way, for every $2 that you make, you must not lose any more than $1. Overall, your goal per trade is to cut your losses to the point that they are only half of what you make by letting your profits run.

If you follow this religiously, you can lose on more than 50 percent of your trades and still make money. That's an important consideration since, statistically speaking, you will probably have more losers than winners in trading. Here's how it works: For ease of illustration, let's say you make 10 trades and you stick to the 2-to-1 rule. On six of your trades—60 percent of the total—you lose $1. On the remaining four trades—40 percent of the total—you make $2. Your losses amount to $6 and your wins total $8. That's a net profit of $2 even though you lost on 60 percent of your trades!

This kind of reward-to-risk ratio can be accomplished only with discipline (there's that word again) and the strict use of stops. If you have a small profit potential with an ultrawide stop your reward-to-risk ratio is totally out of balance. Even if you make money on that trade, you have to question your logic and your execution. If the reward is small, the risk should be even smaller.

Here's what I mean in a real-world example:

Let's say your technical analysis has identified a pivotal area for the S&Ps between 1211.50 and 1212.50. (Remember, this works with any market or stock. We're using the S&P futures index in this example because it's what I trade.) Above that pivotal area, our upside targets at which we'd expect to encounter resistance are 1219, 1222.50, and then 1230.

Now the market has opened, and the initial range is right around that pivotal area, building good support there. So, I go long at 1213, with a stop at 1211, which coincides with the low of the morning opening range thus far. I have a two-point risk to the downside. Now, my upside objective—based on technical analysis—is 1219, or a six-point profit potential. This more than meets my reward-to-risk ratio of risking half as much as I stand to make. Rather, my reward-to-risk ratio is 3:1.

When the market moves higher to 1219 and I exit the trade, I take my six-point profit. It doesn't matter whether the market then moves even higher even though I may miss out on a larger profit. The most important thing is that I executed according to plan. At 1219 I felt that the chance for further upside was diminished. I could have scaled out of the position, but instead I had met my profit objective on this trade. I exited when I felt it made good sense to get out, just as I entered the trade when it made good sense to get in.

Put another way: The goal is to enter trades when the risk of loss is low, and to exit trades when that low-risk threshold is over.

Having a plan and executing it with discipline will help you to determine and carry out the trades that make the most sense. If you know why you're making a trade—old support levels hold, a breakout above key resistance, retracement to a particular level—then you increase the chance of executing it well. The one thing you must avoid is the 50–50 trade (i.e., when the market is equally likely to rise or fall).

Rather, what you're looking for are trades that, once again based on technical analysis, indicate enough potential either on the upside for a long position or to the downside when you go short. If the market could go either way from a particular point, then that's a neutral zone. In this case, it's far better to wait until the market moves to one side of that zone or the other before making a trade.

For example, say the S&Ps have been in a range between 1210 and 1220. (Or a stock might be in a daily range of $48 to $51 over the past several days.) Are you going to buy at 1215? Would you go short at that level? No, you won't because at that point the market could go either way. You'd have only a 50–50 chance of being right, and those aren't odds to trade with. Rather, a better strategy would be to wait until the market goes to 1210.10 or 1210.20, with a sell stop at, say, 1209.80 and a profit target at 1219.50.

As you can see by these previous examples, two trading axioms—a reward-to-risk ratio of 2:1 or better and the use of stops—go hand in hand when it comes to capital preservation. You want your risk to be no more than half of your reward potential. You do this by limiting the losses through the use of stops.

Stops are the safety ropes that keep you from free-falling when the market declines or rises unexpectedly with a move against you. At first, you must be very deliberate about your use of stops. As you plot out your trades, you must identify at the same time the three key points:

1. Entry

2. Exit

3. Stop

Your entry and exit points on every trade will be determined by your technical analysis. You will place your stop so that your reward-to-risk ratio is a minimum of 2:1. Thus, if you're in a position to make four points on a trade, you would not want to risk any more than two points. Remember, the basic tenets of capital preservation work regardless of position size. Whether you are trading 10 S&P majors or one e-mini, or whether you have a position involving 100 shares or 10,000 shares, the discipline remains the same.

But as outlined in Chapter 2, slippage is a fact of life when it comes to trading. You may want to get in the market at a particular price, but with a market order you may get in far above where you wanted to buy or far below where you wanted to sell. At all times you must keep track of the kind of slippage you're experiencing. If it seems excessive, you may want to reexamine how (and with whom) you're entering your orders. Also, slippage must be factored into your trading plan so that your 2:1 reward-to-risk ratio isn't violated. In addition, keep in mind that the bigger you eventually trade, the more slippage will become a problem.

Be aware that stops are where you'd choose to get out of a trade if the market goes against you. But in a very volatile market, you may not be able to exit at exactly where your stop is placed. In other words, just because you have a stop doesn't mean that the stop order will be filled at that price; it may be filled at a higher or lower price because of the prevailing market conditions. That also underscores the inherent risk in trading: If you are undercapitalized and you have a larger than expected loss because your stop was not filled where you expected, you could be out of the game.

Also, keep in mind that you can't just use a mental stop—"If it goes against me I'll get out"—because you'll be tempted not to yank yourself out of the market in time to limit a loss. Because an actual stop order hasn't been entered, you may move that mental stop down further on a losing long position or raise it on a losing short position. Why? Because you believe (or hope or wish or pray) that the market will turn around and go your way. The Ten Commandments in Chapter 1 state there is no "wishing, hoping, or praying" when it comes to the market. Use stops. Period.

How to place stops depends largely on your objective and your style of trading. Essentially, if you are holding a position for several days you most likely will have a wider stop placement than someone who is day trading. In both cases, your stop placement reflects the maximum loss that you can shoulder on one trade.

There is only one time when you should consider moving a stop, and that is when you're using trailing stops. Certainly there are times—as we'll discuss in Chapter 8, "Trading the Nasdaq"—that you may adjust your stop placement. But that occurs as part of your trading plan before you place the trade. What I'm talking about here is the use of trailing stops *during* a trade.

A stop acts much like a safety net. You're 10 feet off the ground, and the net is at 6 feet. When you climb up to 12 feet off the ground, the net is moved up to 8 feet; then you go up to 14 feet and the net is at 10 feet. That's the same concept as trailing stops. These stops move upward with your long position or downward with your short one until you fully exit the trade.

Here's an example:

Your technical analysis indicates support for the S&Ps at 1210. You go long at 1210.10, with an initial profit target—indicated by your technical analysis—of 1215 and a second one at 1220. You place a protective sell stop at 1209. The market moves up to your first target at 1215, and the upward momentum remains strong. So you exit half your position profitably. Now you're still long from 1210.10, headed up to 1220. To keep your risk/reward in balance, you move your stop upward to, say, 1214. That way if the market turns downward before it gets to 1220, you'd still make a profit. If you didn't move the stop and the market turned downward quickly, you'd be stopped out at a small loss at 1209. If you canceled the stop altogether, a drop in the market could wipe out much or all of your profit—and you'd have committed the trading sin of turning a winner into a loser.

As a rule of thumb, you might first raise your stop to the entry point, so if the market turns against you the result would be a "scratch." Then you could raise the stop to protect a profit.

One of the most dangerous moves in the market is to trade without stops. After being stopped out too many times, some traders are tempted not to use them at all. A trader has gone long at 1210, for example, with a stop at 1209. The market goes up to 1211, stalls, then retraces to 1209, at which point the trader is stopped out. The market languishes there for a while, then inches its way up to 1210, and then rallies to 1212.50 and then 1215. Frustrated, the trader sees the stop at 1209 as an impediment that kept him (or her) from having a profitable trade. If it weren't for that stop at 1209, he'd have made a profit. The market did exactly what he thought it would!

The problem is not the stop per se. Rather, once the trader got stopped out, he wasted too much time being emotional—angry at himself and the market—and did not see the potential to get back into the market once it got back above 1210. The real problem, however, comes in placing a trade without a stop. You go long at 1210 and the market inches to 1210.50 and then breaks sharply to 1205. Then you're trying to bail out of a market that's awash with sellers and no buyers. You may not get out until 1203.

As we'll discuss later, if the volatility of the market increases to the point that your stops are being hit too frequently, then you may want to consider widening your stops. But if you do, you must make commensurate reductions in the sizes of your trades. That way, the amount of capital that you expose does not increase.

How large you can trade depends on many variables. One is experience. Even if you have unlimited capital at your disposal, you wouldn't want to jump into trading by buying and selling thousands of shares of stock or 10-contract positions in the S&P majors. Your experience level would dictate small trades as you begin the learning curve.

The amount of money you have *on the line*—not in the bank— determines your risk. Granted, you must focus on the trade and not on the money. But that becomes increasingly difficult when you are trading a larger position than you are inherently comfortable with, given your experience level and the level of volatility in the market.

This brings up the point about paper trading. There is some value to paper trading, in which you go through all the motions of trading—picking your entry, exit, and stop points—without actually making a trade. The best way to paper trade is to record every trade you envision without adjusting it because you meant to do something else. If you keep a log, religiously, of every paper trade through that training phase, you will see where you do well and where you fail. If you consistently get out of a trade too late, for example, you'll have to adjust your methodology for determining exit points.

But paper trading is really just going through the motions. It can't replicate the emotional feeling of trading. For one thing, when you're paper trading your focus is on your entry and exit points. You may decide to enter the market at 1253, and your target is 1256; you watch and wait for the market to go from one point to the other. But when you're trading for real, you'll have to fight a host of emotions from dread to euphoria as the market gyrates in between 1253 and 1256. You'll feel the effect of every tick of the market: relief when it moves from 1253 up to 1253.20, and a sickening fear when it drops from 1254 to 1253.50. Paper trading can't prepare you adequately for that.

Remember, trading is 90 percent emotional and psychological. You won't know what it feels like to risk your capital until you trade for real. Then, and only then, can you learn that balance between too much risk and adequate risk to reap a worthwhile reward. It's a balancing act you'll continue throughout your trading career.

Think of it this way: Two cadets could be at West Point, the esteemed military academy, learning all the same things, from history to strategy to leadership. But you won't know which one will perform the best under fire until they're on the battlefield. On an emotional level, trading is similar. You can look at a chart and pick out the buy and sell points, or you may be able to watch the market in real time. Yet you won't know how you will handle the emotional and psychological pressure of trading until you have committed your capital to your trade—and then successfully made the mental shift to focus on the trade and not the money.

Legends, Language, and Lore of Traders

When I tell this story at conferences or when I give a speech, too many people miss the point. They concentrate on the reward—and miss the lesson about focus and risk. Let's see how well you do.

It was the Thursday after Black Monday, that fateful day in October 1987 when the stock market plunged 502 points. There were many on Wall Street and in the Chicago trading pits who thought it was the end of the world. As I relate in my book, *The Day Trader: From the Pit to the PC* (John Wiley & Sons, 1999), a trading memoir, I was out of the country on Black Monday and rushed back (taking the Concorde from London to New York on standby) to trade. Volatility was huge in those days before there were trading limits, which act as brakes to slow a downward move. The pit looked like a battlefield.

On that Thursday morning, before the opening bell, I scanned the pit. The brokers were acting nervous, anticipating the open. I had been an order filler once, and I knew that edgy feeling. I saw the way they fidgeted, the way their eyes darted about. They were sellers, I decided, and potentially big sellers.

Just before the market opens, brokers are allowed to announce their bids and offers, which sets the tone for the opening. That morning my suspicions were confirmed when a broker shouted out his offer, 400 points lower. Then another broker, this one from Shearson, offered to sell 1,000 points. Remember, there were no trading limits in those days. I wanted to test the water, to see how low this market would go. "I'm 2,000 lower," I roared into the pit.

The Shearson broker answered me back in a second. "I'm 3,000 lower!" (Keep in mind that 3,000 in the pit is equal to 30.00 on the screen. And to illustrate the magnitude of what was happening, a move of 400 or 500 pit points in the S&Ps was a significant move in those days. In the Dow cash market, a 30-point move would have been front-page news. At this point, the S&P futures market hadn't even opened, and we were 3,000 lower.)

I had to know how low it might go. "I'm 4,000 lower!"

The Shearson broker roared back, "5,000 lower!"

With that, S&Ps opened 5,600 points lower. It was a free fall, my

(Continued)

Legends, Language, and Lore of Traders *(Continued)*

gut told me, but it had to be near the bottom. "Buy 'em!" I started to yell to the Shearson broker, but a trader behind me grabbed my arm. "Lewis! I'll see you 150!"

"Buy 'em!" I yelled, and scribbled the trade on my card. I was long 150 contracts with the market about 5,600 points lower.

A second later another broker caught my eye; he was selling 300.

"Can't do it," I signaled back. That would make me long 450 contracts—a huge position in any kind of market, but especially this one. I didn't think I could stomach that kind of risk.

Two seconds later, a trader across the pit caught my attention. "What are you doing?" he signaled.

"I'm a seller," I replied.

I offered those 150 contracts, which I had bought a half-minute before, at 2,000 points higher than my purchase. I made $1.3 million on that single trade. If I'd had those other 300 contracts to sell, my profit would have been a cool $5 million. But I didn't look back.

I had reached my internal risk limit. I made a few other small trades, netting $40,000 or $50,000. Then I'd had enough. Walked out of the trading pit, went into the bathroom, and threw up.

Now, what's the moral of this story? Is it that trading can net you a tidy $1.3 million if you have the intestinal fortitude? Or is it that at all times you can't let the risk overwhelm you? Certainly before this time I had traded hundreds of contracts—but never in a market like this, with a volatility born of crisis and no limits. With the trading curbs now in place, we'll never see anything like it again.

People love this story for the vicarious thrill of making a million in half a minute. But if that's all they hear, they miss the point. The point is about focus that allows you to trade clearheadedly, without taking on risk that will result in panic.

So how much risk is enough, and how much is too much? As your experience and proficiency in making trades increase, you'll increase your trade size. And with that, your profit potential—and your loss potential—will also rise. When is it too much? Once again, you are the best judge. By the time this becomes an issue, you'll know what kind of market suits your trading style the best. You'll know the times of day that you tend to be the most profitable. You'll know the signals and indications of your favorite kind of trade, whether it's playing the breakout or selling the rally. And, you'll undoubtedly favor the long or short side. People usually begin trading by buying. It's natural: You like the setup, so you buy. It's the same with the investing public. If a broker calls an investor and says, "Company X is at $90 and we think it's going down to $50," what's the normal reaction? "Call me when it's at $50 and I'll buy." Rarely will an investor decide to short the stock at $90 with the intention of buying it to cover the short at $50. It's hard for investors to conceive of selling what they don't already own.

For day traders, while the learning curve usually starts out from the long side, there is a point at which they become comfortable going short. Then, it seems that most people like to trade from the short side. There is also a belief out there among traders that the market goes down faster than it goes up. But if you've ever been caught short on a rally, you'll know that the market can skyrocket as quickly as it can plummet.

Whatever your style and preference, when you contemplate increasing the size of your trades, you must consider the "gas tank rule." To give credit where credit is due, this analogy was first told to me by Jim Sebanc, our analyst. It's a good comparison, especially to help new traders understand the concept of forgetting about their capital once they place a trade.

When you drive to the service station and pull up to the pump, you know it will cost you $20 or $30 to fill the tank of your car. You might feel the pinch when you pay, but after you drive away you don't think about the money anymore (although that may get harder to do if the price of gasoline gets to be over $3 a gallon!). It's simply the cost that's necessary to drive your car.

When you trade, you should not think about the money on the line any more than you think about the cost of the gasoline once you drive away from the service station. That capital on the line is simply the cost that's necessary to trade. So if *during the trade* you're thinking about that $500 or $5,000 or $50,000 that you've risked, then you've risked too much. You're trading too large for your risk tolerance and your capitalization.

You know that it takes money to trade. And you know that you're putting money on the line, money that could be lost if the market goes against you. Therefore, if the amount of capital that you risk per trade affects you more than filling your gas tank, then you should reevaluate your trade size in light of your capitalization and risk tolerance.

Once again, capital preservation comes down to discipline and the ability to keep your emotions to a minimum. Your goal is to find a risk level that does not evoke emotion, especially fear, and therefore allows you to stay as objective as possible. When you have that equilibrium, you'll have the best chance of following your game plan to make well-executed trades.

THE WELL-EXECUTED TRADE

That brings us to the second objective of this chapter—the well-executed trade. You can do your analysis. You can target your entry, exit, and stop points. But when do you pull the trigger? If you get in too soon, you could get "chopped around," meaning you'll get stopped out repeatedly and lose capital (and potentially patience) because the market does not have a clear direction. Or you could get in too late, after the move that you've been anticipating has already developed and largely passed you by. If you jump in then, you'll be in danger of chasing the market instead of waiting for the next move.

The key to timing is to know when to trade and when to wait. This means for a given day or in the midst of a particular day. For example, I've learned that if I get caught the wrong way in the market in the morning, between 8:30 and 11:00 A.M. Central time, then I'm better off taking a break. (Yes, even I have to be reminded of my own Commandment of taking a break after a string of losses.) The problem is, when I'm in the pit I'm trading constantly—in and out of scalp trades and scaling into and out of longer-term positions that span a few hours. So if at the end of two hours of grueling trading I have a net loss, I know I'll be further ahead to walk out of the pit, go back to the office, clear my head, take care of the web site business there, and then regroup for the afternoon trading session.

The same thing occurs when I'm trading at the screen. Because of the dynamic of screen trading, I do not typically make as many trades as when I'm in the pit. In other words, I don't do much scalping from the screen. Rather, I do more deliberate day trading, taking a position that may last me from several minutes to an hour or more. But if I end up losing at the end of that morning, I know it's time to take a break. Inevitably, the market will slow down during the midday hours from roughly 11 A.M. until 1:30 P.M. or so Central time. I used to think that it was because all those Wall Streeters were taking two-martini lunches on the East Coast, which corresponded with those slow times in Chicago. And, of course, the traders in the pit do leave for lunch and come back because it's virtually impossible to stand in that pit all day, every day.

Because of this ebb and flow of market activity—Fed announcements and other unexpected events notwithstanding—many traders will sit on the sidelines from the late morning through the noon hour and into the early afternoon. The volume during these times tends to be light, and that light action makes for a perfect environment for fake-outs, when the market rallies higher or breaks lower, and then doesn't have any follow-through. That's why trading during these light-volume times can be frustrating as well as unproductive. Watch the market action, to be sure, but you may find that it suits your trading style better to be on the sidelines.

As a trader, you'll find it's more productive to be involved when the market is more decisive and when strong moves are accompanied by volume. Again, the times for this type of activity are typically in the market opening, up to the first 90 minutes or so, and the market closing, in the last 90 minutes or so.

That's why when 1:30 or 2:00 P.M. Central time rolls around, I'm ready to get back into the market. I sometimes joke that the afternoon session is like *Monday Night Football*. If you lose friendly football wagers on Saturday and Sunday, you still have Monday night to get even! Joking aside, I don't want to draw a parallel between gambling and trading. My point is that traders do tend to look at where they stand at the end of a session of trading. So at the midday break, I know where I stand (was my plan successfully executed or was I off?) and what worked for me and what didn't.

As I enter the afternoon trading session, one of the things I'm looking for is whether the market will retrace some of the moves that it made in the morning or will continue the direction that it has taken thus far.

There is another reason to divide your trading day into two parts. Not only does it help you to focus your trading efforts on those times of the most potential opportunity, it also acts as a kind of antidote to overtrading. Overtrading is often the result of losses that you want to make up for quickly. The root cause, however, is a loss of discipline. You trade too often, too much, too fast, and for too little reason. This is the exact opposite of our goal of the well-executed trade, which is deliberate and based on a host of market criteria that you identified as part of your technical analysis. You go long, for example, because significant support has held. You go short because the buying volume is evaporating at higher levels and overhead resistance is unlikely to be breached. Those are reasons to make a trade. Never trade just for the sake of making a trade. If you do, you'll overtrade your way out of capital and out of the market.

Day traders often look to buy a breakout when the market exceeds a key resistance area that they've identified. The problem is that chances are the breakout has been on many other traders' radar screens as well. Thus, when the market breaks out, there is going to be a lot of emotion in this move. Then as the market moves up, buy stops are going to be hit, which will propel the market even higher. In that case, you're almost assured a poor fill. Slippage may cause you to get in significant higher than you anticipated.

Rather, you may want to wait for that initial euphoria to pass. The market undoubtedly will retrace somewhat and test a level at or near where it staged the breakout. Then if you see buying come in and a base being built, you may have a better chance of a low-risk, high-probability long position.

Another danger to avoid is adding to a losing position. Once again, this is the exact opposite of the goal of the well-executed trade. But knowing what you should avoid will help you to reinforce a better trading behavior.

When a trader adds to a losing position, chances are the problem is a lack of technical research. Most likely, trades are put on without a sound plan behind them. Here's an example. You've been watching a stock—Company X—for a few days. You've missed an up move and now you're kicking yourself. So you jump in, buying at $25.50. What you don't realize, however, is that shares in Company X just entered a resistance area from $25 all the way up through $27. The stock stalls at $25.50 and starts to drift lower. The sellers come in and the stock trades at $25 and then $24.75. You add to the position here, figuring that when it goes back up over $25 you'll sell out for a profit. Instead, the stock continues down to $24.50. You neglected to put in a stop, because you thought the momentum to the upside would continue. You figure that $24.50 has to be a support level, so you buy more. Then more sellers come in because of negative news on another stock in the same sector. Company X is down to $24. Panicked, you buy more because this *has* to be the bottom. You're wishing and hoping that the market will turn around to bail you out of the mess you've created. Instead, Company X keeps moving lower.

This is a misuse of a strategy known as averaging or scaling into a position. When it's part of your plan, averaging is a fine way to get into the market at a variety of prices. For example, if you believe that a market is topping out, you may want to scale into a short position. Or, as the market moves steadily upward, you may want to be a scale-up buyer, going long in small increments until you have established a full position.

But under the scenario just outlined, you're long Company X from $25.50, $24.75, $24.50, and $24. You're relying on hoping, wishing, and praying. (If you don't know what's wrong with that, go back to Chapter 1 and reread the Ten Commandments of Trading.) You stare at the screen, willing the market to move back to $25—or even $24.75. If it does, you'll get out of two positions with a small profit, one for a scratch, and one for a loss. Then you'll breathe a big sigh of relief and—incorrectly—congratulate yourself for getting out of big mess.

It would be far better for the long run for you to get out of this mess by cutting your losses. Yes, at $24 you'd scratch your last trade and lose on all the rest. You'll be kicking yourself for quite a long time, which would actually be the preferable outcome. Why? Because you'll see quickly that adding to a losing position is *not* the way to trade. Scale in and scale out when it's part of your plan, based on technical analysis. Don't just buy because you think the market *has* to be at a bottom or a top. If you think a market just can't go any lower, remember what happened in the tech sector in the first quarter of 2001. Then you know that "can't" just doesn't have much relevance in the market.

At some point along the learning curve, many traders develop a system. Whether they subscribe to a service or they program their own unique criteria, these traders seek to trade via a system that they anticipate will produce low-risk, high-probability trades. In fact, there is an entire school of thought out there in favor of systematic trading. The other school adheres to discretionary trading. Simply put, systematic trading means you trade 100 percent based on your system and the buys and sells it generates. To do that, however, you must make every trade generated. You cannot override your system's recommendations. You must buy when it indicates a buy, and sell when it flags a sell. There will be losing trades among these signals, but if the system is a good one, the profits on the winners will more than offset the losses.

The problem, at least based on personal experience, is that it can be difficult to be a systematic trader. Many traders, myself included, want to be the ones to decide when and how to pull the trigger on trade execution, and also to decide when it's better to wait on the sidelines (such as awaiting an announcement on interest rates) and when to trade. However, if you have a trading system and you override even one trading signal or alter a trade in any way, you have automatically joined the ranks of the discretionary traders.

I have known traders who swore by their systems. But knowing myself and my own trading style, I'm a discretionary trader. You will have to make that call for yourself. But remember, the minute you change a system or fail to take one of the trades that it generates, you are a discretionary trader.

Regardless of whether you're using a system or your own discretion and analysis, the well-executed trade can be broken down into three steps—ready, aim, and fire. In the beginning, these three steps will feel methodical and maybe a little overly deliberate. But in time they will be ingrained in your trading.

1. *Ready:* This is your initial trade setup from clearing your mind of distractions as you mentally prepare to trade to studying your price charts and reviewing your technical analysis. What's your bias for the day? At what price level would you be a buyer and/or a seller, based on support, resistance, and retracements?

2. *Aim:* At this stage, you're watching the market for those setups that you outlined in the first step. Let's say you've identified critical support in a stock or a futures market. The market opens above that level, trades up briefly, then drifts lower. As it nears your support target you tell yourself that it's not going to stay there. You're poised to buy if that happens.

3. *Fire:* This is where it all comes together. You've identified the price levels, and you've taken aim as that setup occurs. Now the target is in your sights. You execute a trade at the price you previously identified, with a protective stop and a first profit target.

That is the essence of the well-executed trade. As you can see, the components are very similar to the steps you take to preserve your capital. In fact, a well-executed trade will take care of much of the concern about preserving capital, and your efforts to preserve capital will go a long way to support your efforts to make a well-executed trade. The common factor in each is balance.

Finally, there is the well-executed trade that goes against you. You've done your research, you've studied the charts, you've followed every step of your trading plan. You execute your trade, with a protective stop to limit your loss and preserve your capital. Then the market goes against you and you're stopped out of a trade. What happened? You went through all three steps of "ready, aim, and fire," and you based it all on a trading plan backed by technical analysis.

First of all, you've still made a well-executed trade. Remember that losses are to be expected in trading. And you can lose on more than half of your trades and still make money if your reward-to-risk ratio is 2:1. Second, it takes a great deal of discipline to deal with a losing trade. If you get out of a losing trade quickly, reevaluate the market, and then trade again, you have indeed successfully made a well-executed trade. It's just that the market didn't do what you expected.

One problem may be the "personality" of the market that you're trading. Your losing trades are your best teachers. So if you consistently have a losing trade due to the same circumstances—you buy a dip and the market breaks, or you buy a rally and it fails—then those losing trades show you that you are out of sync with the market. Your technical analysis and your trading plan then have to be adjusted for the current market dynamics. In other words, you may be playing a breakout market when it's really rangebound. Or you may be trading as if it's rangebound, and the market is trending in one direction or another.

Every trader, particularly in the beginning, finds it easier to follow the market. The market goes up, reaches a high, and starts to fall, so you sell. The market falls, bottoms out, and starts to rise, so you buy. This is buying after the dip and selling after the high.

Or a trader may want to play the breakout. The market reaches a critical resistance area that is wearing down. If it goes through, the next resistance area is the profit target. Or if the market falls to a previous support level and appears likely to extend to the downside, then a trader may want to play the break down.

Experienced traders may combine all these strategies and with varying time frames. For example, I might be bullish overall on the day, but I'll scalp—trading in and out of the market at different price levels—as the market gyrates its way (hopefully) in the direction that I anticipate. Perhaps I'm looking for a breakout move if the market manages to get above a certain price level, but in the meantime I could be trading through a series of fake-outs—buying the bottoms and selling the tops—until the real breakout occurs.

While traders all have their favorite strategies, it's imperative that you pick the best strategy for the market conditions at the time. If you're out of sync with the market it's because you have not yet recognized the "personality" of the market at that time. The quickest way to find out is to look at your losing trades.

I recommend that all traders—novices to professionals—keep logs of their trades. Your log will include the time in, time out, whether you were long or short, and the end result.

The times that you've successfully employed your strategy—whether it's buying the dips/selling rallies or looking for extensions—then you have successfully identified the kind of market you're in. But a rangebound market will eventually break out in one direction or another. A trend will end, and a market will become rangebound. When those changes take place, you have to shift your trading strategy as well.

This ability to read the market and adjust your strategy will help you broaden your trading repertoire. You don't want to be the "one-note Johnny" of trading, only able to buy the dips. You have to be able to trade both the long side and the short side. You want to find the opportunities when the market you're trading is rangebound or it's setting up for a breakout. Once you identify these changes—aided by your technical analysis—then the rest becomes rote memory. Ready . . . aim . . . fire.

6

Intraday Dynamics

The good thing about day trading is that every day is a new day. In fact, every trade is like a fresh sheet in the fiscal ledger. When you focus on the well-executed trade and *not* the money, every trade is a unique, individual transaction that stands or falls on its own. The other part of that scenario is that since every trade and every trading day is unique unto itself, you can't skimp on the preparation. You can't say, "Hey, I studied the charts on Tuesday. This is Wednesday. Nothing's different." Something is always different, even in the most boring, rangebound, sideways-moving market.

Granted, studying the charts is a little like looking at the market in the rearview mirror. You see where it's been and then attempt to determine where it's likely to go next. You may find, for example, that a stock with three lows in a row between $30 and $30.50 will have good support there. Additionally, let's say one of your trend lines comes in at $30.75. So clearly that puts the price area between $30 and $30.75 into the spotlight.

But what actually happens when the market approaches that target area will involve many dynamic factors. Remember, the market doesn't trade in a vacuum. Individual stocks influence the stock index futures. What happens in a particular index—whether it's the Dow, Nasdaq, or S&P or a given sector such as the financials or the techs—will affect individual stocks. And then there are all the announcements and news headlines that can sway the market.

Our goal in this chapter is to examine how to improve your ability to read the market as it develops. This does not in any way lessen the importance of the technical analysis that you do *before* the market opens. Rather, your study of the market cannot end there. Whether you do the analysis yourself or you subscribe to a service or you use a combination of both, you must constantly monitor the market around you.

The intraday dynamics encompass the "aim" part of the three-step process, outlined in Chapter 5, of "ready, aim, and fire." To reiterate, "ready" begins with the mental preparation and culminates with a careful study of the charts and technical analysis. Keep in mind that these intraday dynamics are applicable to both stocks and futures. In fact, the dynamics for the stock index futures—S&P, Nasdaq, and Dow—may be used to trade in these particular markets. In addition, as a stock trader, you will closely watch the dynamics of these indexes to help you with your individual equity trading. As discussed later in this

---

Legends, Language, and Lore of Traders

It had been a very volatile morning in the S&P futures pit, with a steady rally followed by a sharp break. My clerk at the time was a young man we called "Boo." He looked a little rattled as he stood beside me, scanning the crowd.

"Well," he said with a sigh, "the market is either going to go up—or it's going to go down—from here."

"You think so?" I asked him a bit sarcastically.

"Yup," Boo replied. "It's up or down from here."

And with that Boo earned a place in the unofficial history of the market as having made one of the most obvious statements of all time.

But in fairness to Boo, he did capture the essence of intraday dynamics. The market is always going up or down. Even when it's moving mostly sideways, it's still making gyrations in both directions.

chapter, there are other dynamics as well that you will use strictly to assist you with your stock trading. And there will be still other indicators and correlations that you will develop and use over time, particularly as your experience increases and you develop your own system. Our purpose here is to give you an overview of the kinds of intraday dynamics that you should be watching to help you determine when and how to trade in the stock index futures, and to help you analyze the overall market dynamics for your stock trades.

When it comes to broader market sentiment, there are a number of factors to be considered that in total contribute to whether the market—which to the layperson usually means the Dow Jones Industrial Average (the Dow)—is down or up. These factors include news affecting any of the major equities that have a wide sphere of influence—both psychological and fundamental—as well as economic announcements, such as the employment report or consumer confidence report (see Resources), and even developments in overseas markets, such as the political standoff in early April 2001 between the United States and China over the downed U.S. military jet.

To examine these dynamics, let's take a look at Friday, March 30, 2001, which marked the end of the first quarter. It was a tumultuous quarter in the equities market, marked by both the S&P and the Nasdaq futures making one contract low after another and a continuation of the now-fabled "tech wreck" that saw price/earnings (P/E) ratios in some former highfliers burst like soap bubbles. The first quarter of 2001, in fact, was one of the most volatile markets in history, with the Nasdaq falling 25 percent, the S&P 500 dropping 12 percent, and the Dow 8 percent.

Every day on TeachTrade.com, we post a "Morning Meeting," a compilation of our own premarket preparation for that day of trading. Here's an excerpt for Friday, March 30:

S&Ps are trading at 1165.20, higher by 370 points. Bear in mind that this is well above **fair value.** If we open at these levels, it will be 17 points above cash, which is more than double fair value. The single most important thing for traders to be aware of today is that it is the end of a very, very nasty quarter.

What was the setup thus far? S&Ps were above fair value, which is the theoretical relationship between the futures contract and the underlying cash index. It is tracked by institutions and large traders as part of their strategies. But what exactly does that mean for the average trader?

The Chicago Mercantile Exchange describes fair value as an "arbitrage free" level at which futures theoretically should be priced in relation to the cash index values, in the absence of transaction costs. Fair value typically reflects the cash or "spot" index value (such as the S&P 500 cash index or SPX), plus financing charges (reflecting current prevailing interest rates), less any dividends that would accrue and be paid on the stocks in the underlying index. (Once the dividends are paid on the underlying stocks, the cash index goes down by the aggregate amount of the dividends.)

Thus, fair value does not change intraday. Rather, fair value—based on this mathematical formula of time, money, and dividends—is calculated daily, representing what the relationship of futures and cash should be, minus any market factors. However, futures may trade above (at a premium) or below (at a discount to) fair value intraday. In other words, futures may be at a higher premium to cash than the normal fair value. Or futures may be at a discount of fair value.

What this tells you *at the opening* is that the market is out of equilibrium. That's going to set up some opportunities for large players—the arbitrageurs who try to trade on the difference between the cash and futures—to trade. But that opportunity, often in the form of program trading, is going to be rather short-lived. In other words, we could see a choppy open—as futures are sold and stocks are bought, or vice versa—until fair value comes in line.

For the average trader, however, fair value is probably of most use as a speculative sentiment indicator. For example, if speculators/traders think the market is going higher, they will pay more than fair value. Thus, in general terms, when futures are below fair value it's a bearish indicator, and when futures are above fair value it's bullish. But keep in mind that the market won't stay above or below fair value for very long because trading programs that take advantage of such anomalies will bring it back in line—unless, of course, there has been an exceptional event such as a surprise rate cut (or hike) by the Fed or a major news announcement.

The second thing we noted in our Morning Meeting commentary was that March 30 was the end of the quarter. You can't trade in a vacuum, using your charts alone. You have to know what other factors would likely influence the market that day. Is an important economic report coming out, such as the National Association of Purchasing Management (NAPM) report or the employment report? (See Resources.) Is Federal Reserve chairman Alan Greenspan testifying before Congress, as he often does? If so, what's his topic? Will it be something benign in market terms, such as the balance of trade, or will he possibly make a comment about monetary policy?

In this example, since it was the last trading day of the quarter, we knew that portfolio managers would likely adjust their holdings. While that buying or selling would be separate from the dynamics of the market, it would still have an impact. What we had seen in the previous days was heavier buying in the financial and other defensive equity sectors than market conditions would have otherwise warranted. The tech sector, already under pressure, saw some more selling that was related to portfolio adjustments.

What did that mean to traders on March 30? "We would expect it to be a very choppy and light-volume trade," the Morning Meeting stated. In other words, we expected spurts of activity in the stock index futures markets, but a lack of follow-through—in one direction or the other.

Then it was time to look at the numbers. We had identified over the past few days a key level of resistance in S&P futures at 1168 to 1171.50. "We have seen excellent two-way trade up in this area," the Morning Meeting stated, meaning both buyers and sellers had been active in this zone.

The market typically trades back to levels where it has experienced high activity. In other words, if there was a lot of activity—both buying and selling—at a certain price level in a stock or a futures contract, chances are good that the market will return to that price level. That was a price level at which—for whatever reason—both buyers and sellers were willing to commit to a trade. Barring a dramatic change in market sentiment, if that price level is reached again, it would likely produce more trading activity.

What else does that 1168 to 1171.50 area tell us? At the point the Morning Meeting was posted (at approximately 8:15 A.M. Central time), S&Ps were trading at 1165.20 on Globex. Keep in mind that the S&P majors trade overnight on Globex, the Merc's electronic order-matching system, until shortly before the opening of the morning session. That Globex level gives a fairly good indication of where the market is likely to open.

Since we were below the key level of 1168 to 1171.50, that would be significant overhead resistance. And, should the market get above that level, it would obviously turn to support. More importantly, 1168 to 1171.50 would be a key transition zone at which the market would "make up its mind" about its future direction.

Remember, as traders we trade what the market presents to us. We don't set up a trade and then wait for the market to move in one way or the other. Nor do we decide that buying dips is the best strategy for us, and therefore we're going to buy dips all day. You trade the market as it unfolds, based on your technical analysis and what you observe intraday.

As a trader, when I look at a chart I see a course of action. When I trade—in the pit or at the screen—I refer to this course of action to help me define the price levels at which I'll want to be long or short. For me, that course of action is like a map. Of course, there may be some unexpected obstacles along the way that throw the market off course. But I don't let them distract me. Usually we'll get back on course. Or, in the case of an unexpected event or surprise announcement, we'll chart another course.

That's where the intraday analysis comes in. At TeachTrade.com, we post these in the form of "Market Updates." Using our Morning Meeting commentary as a "course of action," we give the play-by-play of what we see happening around us in the market. This real-time commentary—which is the same analysis we do for our own trading—reflects the intraday dynamics that all traders must watch and analyze for themselves. Some of these dynamic factors will weigh more heavily on the market than others, depending on the day.

Let's examine another excerpt from that March 30 Morning Meeting commentary. We noted that if S&Ps could settle above 1168 to 1171.50, it would "bode well for the market." But what would happen then? Our indicators and analysis pinpointed other targets for that day, namely "light resistance" between 1176 and 1177.

"If we can get above 1180 to 1181, there is a good chance that we'll fill the leftover gap at 1192." Gaps are created on a chart when the market opens significantly higher or lower versus the previous trading day's close. That gap then becomes a target, making one of the most popular day trades, the filling of the gap.

Markets fill open gaps about 90 percent of the time, often the day they are created, but commonly within two days. The few times that gaps are not filled usually result in a strong, significant move in the same direction of the gap. For example, on March 12, 2001, S&Ps gapped 12 points lower on rumors in the market of potential Japanese bank failures. The gap was never filled that day, and S&Ps finished the day down about 53 points.

Referring back to the Morning Meeting, we have noted the targets for the upside. Now, let's look to the downside. Should the market move lower, we would expect it to pause or potentially to stop at specific levels of support. And since the market likes to test these levels— to see if support will hold stop a move—you would want to watch the trade activity there. From the perspective of a course of action, you would plot both the resistance and support levels as prices at which you would contemplate establishing a long or short position—depending on other corroborating market conditions.

The March 30 Morning Meeting noted that there was support between 1158 and 1161, and if that level were breached we'd expect a trade down to 1150. On the previous day, S&Ps had traded briefly into the 1140s, with a session low for March 29 of 1144. What that told us on March 30 was that any trade back into the 1140s—a level that was traded only briefly on March 29—would be a negative to the market. Additionally, we knew that if the market settled below 1150, it would be an even greater negative for the upcoming week.

What happened on March 30? S&P futures opened at 1161.30, traded over that key zone at 1168–1171.50, with a high of 1177, which we had targeted as a light resistance area. (Our intraday low was 1152. We had stated that a trade down to 1150 was likely if we failed to stay above 1158 to 1161.) Our settle for that day was at 1169.20, right in the midst of that key zone.

As with everything else in trading, and in life, there will be days when you will be more on target than others. You can't possibly expect to be correct 100 percent of the time, or even most of the time. Rather, you continuously analyze the market, reevaluate conditions, and adjust your strategy based on the intraday dynamics. While our example was for S&P futures, the same concepts apply to any traded market—whether an individual stock or a futures contract. And, as we'll discuss later in the chapter, if you're trading stocks exclusively you must be aware of the dynamics within the broader market. What happens in the Nasdaq 100 futures market, especially when it comes to market sentiment, will have an impact—directly or indirectly—on the individual Nasdaq 100 issues that you're trading.

FROM THE OPENING

Intraday dynamics begin right at the opening. Granted, it could take a while for the market to determine its overall direction for the day. But it's still important to see where the market opens, particularly with regard to certain key price levels.

Once trading is underway, the point to watch is the opening range. That becomes the first reference point for the day. Now, let's say the market at midmorning trades below that opening range, then comes back and breaks through that range to the upside. This would be a good indication that there is upside momentum building that may lead to a rally. Why? For one thing, the opening range was breached to the downside, but the market did not keep going lower.

The opening range becomes the focal point for your trading dynamics. At any given time, you must know where the stock and/or index that you're trading is in relation to the opening range. Also, the opening range could be the high for the day, or be the bottom for that session, or be roughly at the 50 percent point. That will also color the trading dynamics, adding to the bearish, bullish, or neutral sentiment at any given moment. Thus, along with trend lines, moving averages, and other indicators that you may be using to guide your trading decisions, you must also keep the opening range on your radar screen.

One example of how the opening range can be used as a pivotal area is with a stop-reversal strategy. A stop reversal is used, in this case, to exit a losing trade and to enter a new trade because you believe the market sentiment or dynamics has shifted. Let's say the market is trading below the morning range, which you believe has now become significant resistance. You initiate a short position with a buy stop—to get you out of the short position—just above the morning range. In addition, you believe that should the market rally above the opening range, you'll want to be long from that level. Using a stop reversal, you would cover your short position above the morning range, and also get long from that point. Once again, the use of the stop reversal will reflect your technical analysis and your belief about the underlying market sentiment.

In addition to the opening range, there are other pivotal areas that emerge in the market based on previous trading activity. For example, on TeachTrade.com, we often highlight a pivotal area above which the market has a better chance of moving to the upside and below which the market would likely move to the downside.

Most commonly, these are price levels at which we've seen a good two-way trade (both buying and selling) in previous sessions or overnight. We also use proprietary techniques to help us determine these pivotal levels. What you as a trader will look for are those areas with strong volume on previous trading days, or at which the market traded for an extended period of time.

For example, in our April 9, 2001, commentary, we identified 1145 as a pivotal level, comparing it with an "on/off switch." Above this level, we favored the long side; below it, we favored the short side. This level was targeted based on a variety of indicators and trend lines, some of which are part of our proprietary analysis. (We share the results of the analysis in our market commentary posted on TeachTrade.com, but not the methodology for deriving it.)

THE HOURLY CLOSE

Beyond the opening range, one of the factors watched in intraday trading is the hourly close. Typically, prices at the close of each 60-minute interval are charted. The easiest way to see this is with candlestick charts. The pattern of the chart then gives an indication of the trend in the market—upward, downward, or rangebound.

As an example, we'll discuss hourly closes for the S&P market. Trading begins at 8:30 A.M. Central time. Thus, the first hour will close at 9:30, the second at 10:30, and so on. Other closes that are watched include 30-minute and 45-minute closes.

Whatever your parameters, let's say that as the day progresses, a candlestick chart shows a progressively higher pattern. The candles have well-defined bodies formed by the difference between the open of that bar and the close. The candles have "needles" or "tops," which are the spikes above the candlesticks that show the high of that period. And they have "tails" or "bottoms," which are the spikes below that show the lows.

A classic upward pattern looks like a staircase, indicative of a market that is moving higher. The opposite pattern indicates a market moving lower. For example, see the staircase pattern formed midday on the intraday Dow cash chart in Figure 6.1.

A candlestick that has no body at all, but is all needle or tail, is called a "doji." (For example, see the two dojis on the one-month chart for BEA Software (BEAS) in Figure 6.2.) A doji is formed when the open and close of the bar are the same or virtually the same. This kind of formation is often indicative of a trend reversal, especially if the market has already shown a clearly defined pattern. Thus, a doji often appears at the top or the bottom of a particular move.

This kind of pattern analysis can be applied to any chart and any given time frame. The hourly close, however, is widely used by traders, and thus these particular price levels do tend to act like magnets for activity.

For example, in our Mid-Day Updates on TeachTrade.com, you might read that the S&Ps need to close above a particular price level on an hourly basis for an uptrend to be intact. Or we might say they

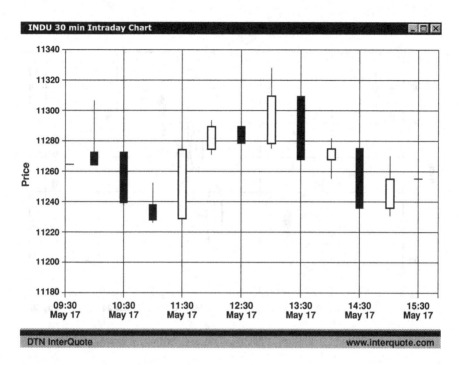

Figure 6.1 INDU 30-Minute Intraday Chart (Dow Jones 30 Industrials) (*Source:* www.interquote.com, DTN Financial Services)

need to close below a certain level on an hourly basis for a downtrend to continue. What we're indicating is that at the close of the next 60-minute interval—based on what we've seen thus far—we would expect the market to behave in a certain way.

RETRACEMENTS

One of the significant price levels you'll watch intraday are retracements of previous up and down moves. Just as with the trend lines we drew in Chapter 4, the retracements can be based on just about any measurable move. But typically, we look at retracements of significant moves—from a contract high to a contract low or from a monthly high closing to a monthly low closing. These retracement levels act like

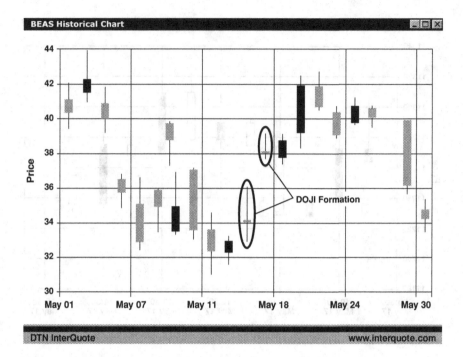

Figure 6.2   BEAS Historical Chart (Daily) (BEA Systems Inc.) (*Source:* www.interquote.com, DTN Financial Services)

magnets. The market tends to seek out these price levels. Maybe that's because these retracements are fairly commonly used by traders and therefore become even more significant because the majority is watching them.

Whatever the reason, specific points along the retracement path are noted by most traders. Whether you incorporate them in your trading system or not, it's important to know where they are since so many other traders are looking at these price points. In general, think of these retracements as significant points the market is likely to gravitate toward. Or these retracement targets could be the point at which a move stops or even retraces.

Retracements commonly looked at are 25 percent, 33 percent, 50 percent, 66 percent, and 75 percent. These progressions—quarter, third, half, two-thirds, and three-quarters—are natural points along the way of a major move. Using these percentages, you can calculate significant retracements of a particular move—particularly as these targets come into view. For example, let's say a stock has had a significant run-up in price from $25 to $45 a share over a six-week period. When the stock is at the high of $45 a share, some negative news comes out that impacts this company and its entire sector. It starts to decline, from $45 down to $40 a share. At that point, it has retraced 25 percent of the up move from $25 to $45 a share. At $35 a share it has retraced 50 percent of the move, and at $30 it has retraced 75 percent.

One of our favorite retracements is 88 percent. This percentage, we have found over time, often marks the end of a significant move. Let's say we're long the S&Ps from 1215. The market moves up to 1230. However, we have identified 1235 as roughly an 88 percent retracement of a previous down move from 1245 to 1163. That puts 1235 squarely in our sights as a target. Thus, at 1230 we might be likely to remain long with at least a portion of our position in anticipation that the market would move toward 1235. However, we'd look for other indicators to confirm that probability—such as strong buy volume and strength in the other indexes, especially the Dow and Nasdaq. If the indicators were decidedly bullish, we might even add to the position at 1230, looking for a move up to 1235.

The absolute end of the run may not prove to be 1218.60. The market could top out at a 90 percent or 91 percent retracement. But the risk of hanging on for a few more ticks would far outweigh the possible rewards, particularly if the market should reverse suddenly and make getting out of a position troublesome.

Remember, your goal as a trader is to execute a trade when the risk is low and the probability of success is high. You exit the trade when the low-risk period is over and the probability of continuation of the move in your direction becomes slight.

In addition to the percentages just outlined, there are other retracement levels that traders often look at, namely 38.2 percent and 61.8 percent, as well as 50 percent mentioned earlier. These are Fibonacci retracements, named after a European mathematician who studied number series in the twelfth century. He came up with his series by adding a first number to a second, the second to the third, and so on

(1, 1, 2, 3, 5, 8, 13, 21 . . .). This became known as the Fibonacci series, which has been applied to architecture, plants, the human body,
and, of course, the market. And in the study of Fibonacci series, two
percentages are commonly used: 61.8 percent and 38.2 percent,
which are also applied to retracements in the market.

Once again, whether you discount Fibonacci retracements or you
swear by them, it will be helpful to know where these retracement levels are in the market. Because even if they aren't a part of your trading
system, enough traders may be watching and using them to make
these retracement levels significant.

But consider what happened on April 5, 2001, as the market rallied
on some positive news from Dell Computer. ("U.S. Stocks Power
Ahead, Dell Sparks Buying Spree," Reuters, April 5, 2001.) At
roughly noon Central time, Nasdaq futures (NDM) set a new session
high for that day at 1496. As we posted in the Mid-Day Updates on
TeachTrade.Com:

> The trade has been a very solid grind higher, led by MSFT [Microsoft],
> which now accounts for over 10 percent of the index, and is up nearly 4
> on the day. In addition, we have had solid performance in the second
> tiers and just about anything else you can name. . . . From 1507 to 1517
> we have the open from [April 3], the high from [April 3], the settle and
> low from [April 2] encompassed by this zone. . . . Also, 1517.90 is a
> 61.8 percent [retracement] of the weekly range.

This confluence of factors—the key price points from April 2 to
April 3 and the 61.8 percent retracement—highlights the importance of
1517.90 as a target. As a trader studying intraday dynamics, that would
put this price level on your radar screen, both as a target and as a price
level at which to observe trade activity as a hint to future direction.

SWING HIGH/SWING LOW

Other chart formations to watch for, both intraday and over the course
of several days or even weeks, are the "swing high" and the "swing

low." A swing high is formed when the market moves up to a high and then trades off sharply. This leaves a spike high with a lower market on either side. Conversely, a swing low is formed when the market moves to a low and then trades higher sharply. This leaves a spike low with a higher market on either side.

Looking at a chart, identify swing highs and the swing lows. Now, by drawing horizontal lines through these points, you can identify support and resistance levels for the market. Further, when these resistance/support levels coincide with a retracement, the importance of the price level is underscored.

STAIRCASES

Remember, the market tends to have symmetry, as we explored in Chapter 3. In the most basic sense, a gradual up move would be reflected by a gradual down move, although the "start" and "stop" points may not be exact. Another kind of symmetry that you could expect in the market is the staircase.

A "staircase" is formed when the market trades to a level, stops, then trades to the next level. This works on both the upside and the downside. The pattern, however, is for successive moves that, when charted, look just like steps on a staircase. Therefore, if the market makes a staircase move, we'll say to the downside, on one day, the likelihood increases for a similar-style move to the upside. Put another way, if the market has a staircase move down, if a rally were to occur the next day, it's unlikely it would be an explosive move to the upside. Rather, the same kind of staircase move would be likely on the upside, as well.

In addition to these examples of intraday dynamics, you must watch for the patterns—such as wedges and triangles—as they form, as well as the intramarket dynamics. There are days when the Dow might be bolstering the S&P, or the tech-dominated Nasdaq might be dragging down the entire market. These factors will influence your trading of individual stocks as well as the broader indexes.

LIMITS

Before the infamous crash of 1987, stocks—and stock index futures—
were allowed to trade without limits. But in the crash and the days that
followed, there was concern, particularly in regulatory circles, that a
free fall could do massive damage, economically and psychologically,
in the market. Thus, limits were born.

For example, on the New York Stock Exchange (NYSE), there are
"circuit breakers" that are meant to "reduce volatility and promote investor confidence" (NYSE Regulation, www.nyse.com), by limiting
trading—and sometimes temporarily halting trading—after significant
moves. Similarly, the Chicago Merc has limits in its stock index futures contracts, the S&P and Nasdaq. These limits were adopted as
part of a "compromise" that kept the regulators in Washington, DC,
from imposing severe limitations on the futures exchange following
the crash of 1987.

The limits are regularly adjusted for prevailing market conditions.
The most current limits are posted on the Chicago Merc's web site at
www.cme.com. (See Resources—Useful Web Sites.) As of this writing (July 12, 2001), the S&P major and e-mini contracts have a first
limit of 55 percent or, as of this writing, 60 points in the S&Ps. The
second limit comes in at 10 percent or 120 points. The Nasdaq major
and e-mini contracts have a first limit of 5 percent or 90 points and a
second limit of 10 percent or 180 points. The points for each limit are
readjusted at the end of each quarter. Thus, if the S&Ps settle at 1200,
the first limit down on the next trading day would be at 1140 and the
second limit would be at 1080. If Nasdaq settled at 1700, the first limit
down would be 1610 and the second limit would be 1520.

In theory, limits act like brakes to slow a downward move. But in
reality, I believe they often act like targets, at least psychologically.
For that reason, I'm in the camp that doesn't like trading limits (and I
remember the days when we didn't have them). Limits, in my opinion,
introduce an element of artificiality to the markets. If the pure dynamics are enough to cause, say, a 30 point move in S&Ps, then the market
should be allowed to trade to that level unimpeded. That, however, is
not the case.

Limits exist to give the market a chance to catch its collective breath. No more free falls. No 5,600-point down moves at the open, as on the opening on the Thursday following the crash of 1987 (see Chapter 5). Yet as I mentioned, limits do become targets. It's part of the "how low can it go?" mentality that traders in the market sometimes adopt. For example, let's say that S&P futures are trading at 1211 and limit down comes in at 1208. As long as the bearish sentiment continues, you know that 1208 is going to be a target. Traders will try to push the market down with selling to see if that 1208 limit down can be set off.

Once a limit offer has been established, trading can occur only *at or above* this limit for 10 minutes, or until 2:30 P.M. Central time. At the end of the 10 minutes, if the contract has remained offered at the limit price for the entire 10 minutes then trading will halt for 2 minutes. Trading will then resume with the second limit in effect.

Once a futures contract is offered limit down, the most important factor is the cash price. It is critical for a trader to know exactly where the cash was trading when the limit was hit in the futures contract. So, while you are unable to trade the futures (which have "locked limit"), you can see the fluctuations in the underlying cash market. You can discern from the activity in the cash market if the limit in the futures was caused by widespread selling or just a single seller in the futures who moved the market lower, meaning it will likely bounce back after the limit expires.

If the futures are limit down and cash starts to tick higher, odds are that the futures will come off the limit (meaning trading above that limit) *before* the 10 minutes have passed. Watching the cash market is critical to knowing how the futures will trade off the limit.

Here's an example of a very common trade based on limit-down prices. Let's say a futures contract is held at the limit price for the entire 10 minutes that the limit is in effect and then opens below the limit. Traders often expect the market at some point to bounce back to the limit price. Therefore, it is very common to see buying after a futures contract comes off the limit (meaning the limit is lifted after the 10 minutes pass).

As you've read thus far, trading is far from an exact science. Often it's a string of probabilities put together, such as if this, this, and this happen, then we're likely to see that occur. Rarely does a move occur because of just one thing. A key stock or group of stocks may go positive, bolstering a sector such as the Semiconductors index (SOX), and then providing strength to the Nasdaq, which then leads a rally in the S&P.

As traders we tend to focus narrowly on whatever we're trading, whether it's S&Ps or a handful of stocks. But each stock and index is part of the overall market. While there will be variances—certain sectors may be up one day while other sectors are down—it's important to remember that there is truly one market overall, with interrelated parts that may move in concert with each other or contrary to each other.

As traders, our task is to analyze as many factors *as is practical.* Notice I did not say "as many factors as possible," because that can contribute to a common trader downfall known as "information overload." You watch every indicator, chart, bar, candlestick, and trend line. You observe all the indexes and subindexes, key indicator stocks, and scrolling news headlines, and you have one of the all-financial-news television stations droning in the background. The problem is sorting through what can be conflicting information to focus on what's important. Otherwise, you can be so lost in the data input that you are unable to execute a trade.

Once again, the goal is balance. You must have enough information to trade, but you can't have so much that it drowns you. Over time and with experience, you'll know what indicators work best with your style and your trading system, as well as what you must always focus on and what you can safely ignore. Overall, as you study your indicators and trend lines in a dynamic format, you cannot focus only on certain target prices. Rather, you want to study the behavior of the market at those price levels.

Here's an example. You may believe that 1650 is key resistance in the Nasdaq futures. We'll say the market has topped out there three times in the past four trading sessions. Now, it's approaching 1650 once again. You're absolutely correct that 1650 is a price level to watch. But you can't assume that just because that level capped previous up moves it will automatically do so again. Rather, you must watch the behavior of the market up to and at the price. Does the buying dwindle as the market nears 1650? Or is the buying steady, as if the market has enough momentum to take it up to and possibly through 1650? If it trades at and above 1650, are there still strong bids from buyers? Or do the sellers take over at that level?

Focus on the market behavior—not just the price level.

FADE TRADE

Now that we've explored some of the more common intraday dynamic factors, let's take a brief look at how some of these indicators might be put into practice as part of a trade. Once again, we're looking at factors such as the opening range, pivotal areas, and how the market behaved at various price points.

Let's say our analysis had identified a key level in the Nasdaq of 1520, a price at which we had seen a strong two-way trade over the past two sessions. Now, the market opens well below 1520 and has difficulty reaching this critical zone in the first few minutes. Finally, it hits 1520 but can't go higher; instead it declines. At this point, you can deduce that the downside is still dominating. The market had difficulty reaching 1520, and once it did, it had a reversal to the downside.

How would you try to capitalize on that move? First of all, 1520 would be your target. The market opening well below it would probably have given you a bearish bias, which would be confirmed by the struggle that the market had to get to that price level. You'd be looking for a place to get short, figuring that the odds still favored the downside, particularly as you approached the 1520 target.

So to fade this up move, you'd look to get short at or around 1520. Fading means that you are doing the opposite of the market because you believe that it will quickly run out of steam and reverse. In this case, while the market is moving higher, you'd be looking to fade with a short position to capture what you anticipate will be a move to the downside.

Remember, it's never wise to try to pick an exact top or bottom. But that's the beauty of a fade trade. If you believe a move—we'll say to the upside—is likely to run out of steam *at or around* a particular target, you may fade that move by getting short *at or near* a price target. Or, you could scale into a short position, meaning you might sell at several successive price levels approaching a target. At the target, if reached, you'd take on the last portion of your position.

There are other factors that play into the decision to fade a move or look for an extension. Among them are volatility and volume. There are times when the market has both low volume and low volatility. When the market is in a tight range and trade participation is light, it would be unlikely that we'd see range extensions of any substance. In other words, there would be a decided lack of participation, enthusiasm, and volume to take the market beyond its existing range.

That's usually a good setup for fade trades between old highs and old lows. Let's say a certain price has been established as the top of a range in a stock or a futures market. The market has hit there two or three times in recent days, but never broken through. You determine that the bottom of the range is solid support. Thus the top and the bottom of the range are well-established and defined.

In this scenario, with low volume and low volatility you'd expect this stock or index to stay within that range. And if it were to break out, say to the upside, it would most likely have difficulty sustaining higher levels.

But there are always the exceptions. There are some times when a move can happen on light volume. In the S&Ps, this kind of activity is particularly noticeable in the trading pit. You can see—and hear—independent, local traders trying to make something happen. That's fertile ground for a "fake-out."

FAKE-OUT

In the trading pit, the signs of a fake-out are obvious. There is a rise in the noise level as traders shout their bids and offers. The price rises—

or falls—to a specific target. Then it reaches the target, maybe trades a touch higher (or lower, depending on the direction of the move). And then . . . nothing. With no follow-through, the market drifts in the other direction.

On the screen, it's easy to see a fake-out—in retrospect, that is. Figure 6.3 is an example from March 20, 2001, the day the Federal Reserve announced a 50-basis-point cut in rates, and a disappointed market (that had hoped for 75 points) reacted with a much lower case.

As we'll discuss shortly, there are times when the market will be ripe for a fake-out, such as after a Fed announcement. But there are other times to be aware of the possibility of a fake-out when you're trading at the screen. Let's say the market has been moving slowly all day and volume has been particularly light. The market

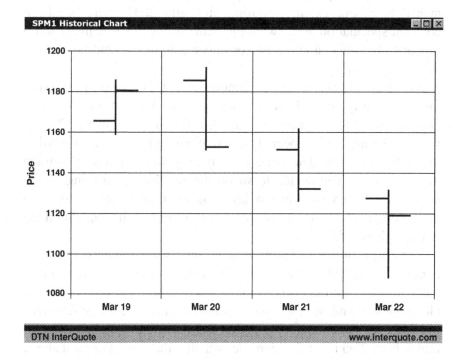

Figure 6.3 SPM1 Historical Chart, March 20, 2001 (*Source:* www.interquote.com, DTN Financial Services)

approaches a key area, but doesn't go any higher. With a lack of participation, the market will either reverse quickly or start to drift lower.

The lower it goes, the more the market could accelerate to the downside. There will be those who bought the breakout to the upside, thinking it was the real thing. Now they are scrambling to get out and reduce their losses. If the market hits sell stops, that will intensify the downward move.

Fake-outs will happen. Unfortunately, the only sure way to tell if a move was a fake-out is when it's all over. But to prepare yourself, you should know that there are times, as alluded to earlier, when the market is more likely to have a fake-out. In addition to low-volume days, you should be on the lookout for a fake-out when the market is awaiting a report or announcement, particularly if it has some emotion attached to it. For example, throughout early 2001, there has been constant speculation about what the Federal Reserve was likely to do to ward off a recession, boost consumer confidence, and bolster the market in the process.

Each time the Fed makes an announcement, fake-outs are so common that we typically look for them on that day and into the next. Only after a day or so does the true direction usually emerge. This is because the market is especially reactive during these times. Knowing this will help you to determine your strategy, whether you try to trade the fake-out or you decide to sit on the sidelines until things settle down. Whatever your decision, knowing when fake-outs are likely to occur can go a long way to preventing you from getting caught on the wrong side of a fake-out.

Regardless of the backdrop of news and announcements, you must continue the technical analysis that started your day. You must continually monitor not only where the market is, but also how it reacted along the way and what that means in the context of the past few trading days. It's not enough to note that the market has returned to an intraday high. You must also consider whether the market opened above or below the previous high. What is volume like? Is there follow-through at the high? Or are the buyers disappearing?

STOCK TRADING DYNAMICS

At the risk of oversimplifying, it's important to remember that prices go up when demand outstrips supply, and prices go down when supply is greater than demand. In individual stocks, that's visually represented by time and sales—a running record, based on time, of when trades are made and at what price. In addition, using a Level II screen you'll be able to see who is dominating the action at the moment—the buyers or the sellers. But you can't trade an individual equity in a vacuum. A variety of intraday dynamics are affecting prices and the perceptions of the buyers and sellers. For example, if buyers believe that the supply of low-priced shares of a particular stock is going to be depleted, they'll step up to buy aggressively. Conversely, if sellers believe that demand for high-priced shares of a particular stock is going to ease, they'll increase the selling pressure.

Now, put that in a larger perspective, looking beyond the equity you have on your radar screen to the broader market. In fact, as an equity trader you will always want to know where the stock indexes are trading. This is a quick gauge of market sentiment and, potentially, an indication of future direction.

At a minimum, if you trade Nasdaq equities, you'll want to have the Nasdaq Composite on your screen, as well as the Nasdaq 100 futures, which may be one of the best indicators of stock price movement for Nasdaq 100 stocks and the tech sector as a whole. In addition, you'll want to know how the S&P 500 cash and futures are trading, as well as the Dow cash. You may also want to monitor other indexes, such as the Semiconductor index (SOX), which often correlates with movements in the Nasdaq 100, and the Banking index (BKX), which may be moving in concert with the S&Ps.

Direct-access trading screens can be configured with multiple windows or views to display a variety of information. Keep your computer screen, or desktop, free of unrelated clutter. Have the most vital information at your fingertips. At a minimum, as a direct-access trader, you'll want to have a Level II screen for the stock that you're actively trading—or multiple Level IIs if you're active in more than one equity. In the beginning, stick with the more actively traded equities with good volume that move in comparatively small increments. A stock that moves from 50 to 50.125 to 50.25 to 50.375 and then back down again will allow you to plot and carry out your trades. The danger, particularly for a newbie, is the thinly traded equity that jumps around on low volume. For example, a stock that moves from 10 to 11 to 12 to 11 and back to 12 without much activity in between those price points will chop you up and severely limit your ability to carry out a well-executed trade.

On the Level II screen, you'll focus on two sources of market information: current bids and offers or asks and the time and sales. Let's take them one at a time. The bids and offers show you exactly which market maker or ECN is active in a stock and at what price. On the left is the list of buyers who want to buy a particular stock, and the list of bid prices, starting with the highest. On the right is the list of sellers who are willing to sell this stock and a list of prices, starting with the lowest. When there is a spread between the bid and the ask, professional market makers may try to capitalize on that differential by buying at the bid and selling at the ask. That difference may only be an eighth, but when large quantities of stock are involved, that can be a significant profit opportunity.

For you, the retail stock trader, the bid/ask arbitrage is probably more of an information tool than a profit opportunity. Looking at the bid and ask prices—and how the stock is trading—will give you an indication of support, resistance, and trend.

For example, let's say you're looking at Company X. On your Level II screen, you see bids and offers as in Table 6.1. (On an actual Level II, you will see the name of the market maker, such as LEHM for Lehman or MLCO for Merrill Lynch, or a particular ECN such as ISLD for Island or ARCHIP for Archipelago. Size is expressed in hundreds; thus 5 is 500 and 10 is 1,000 shares.)

Looking at this hypothetical display of bids and offers, you'll see that there are several buyers willing to pay $30.125, and several sellers at $30.25. The price will move based on the activity that takes place in the market. For example, if the buying (demand) is in excess of the stock that is for sale (supply) at that price, then the stock must

Table 6.1   Level II Screen

Name	Bid	Size	Name	Ask	Size
Market maker A	30.125	10	Market maker E	30.25	10
Market maker B	30.125	10	Market maker F	30.25	10
ECN 1	30.125	20	ECN 4	30.25	5
ECN 2	30.125	5	ECN 5	30.50	10
Market maker C	30.00	1	Market market G	30.50	8
Market maker D	30.00	3	ECN 6	30.75	5
ECN 3	30.00	10	ECN 7	30.75	5

go up to the next level. Conversely, the buyers will get their low price if sellers (supply) are willing to sell at that price.

Looking at this price action, you'll see that baseline of bids that indicates support. If buyers exhaust the supply at, say, $30.125, and must move up to $30.25, then you know support is being built in at $30.125. Similarly, if buyers back away at high price levels, sellers must lower their offers; then that higher price becomes resistance. You can also view this on a chart. The bars and charts you see forming are based on what you're looking at in real time on a Level II screen.

Also on your Level II, you'll see the time and sales for a given equity. The prices scroll real-time, recording the trade price and the amount. For example, you might see 30.125 100, 30.125 50, 30.125 10. That means 10,000 shares (100 times a factor of 100) traded at $30.125 a share, then 5,000 shares at $30.125, and another 1,000 traded at $30.125. The next time and sales might be at 30.00 20 and 30.00 10. This means that 2,000 shares sold at $30 and then 1,000 shares sold at 30. On your screen, this second set of prices at 30 would be in red, since it is below the earlier set of prices at 30.125. Had the second set been higher at, say, 30.25, these prices would have been displayed in green.

In addition to the real-time bid and ask prices and the time and sales, you'll be plotting your strategy using charts that show support, resistance, trends, and moving averages. (See Chapters 3 and 4.) Your own style and preferences will determine the kinds of trades you're making in equities. But in general, day trading of equities should be undertaken only by those who are watching the market full-time with a variety of indicators.

Your technical analysis may indicate solid support or strong resistance, which may take more than one day to be realized. That kind of short-term position trading is known as "swing trading." This type of trade may be undertaken by full-time traders and professionals who are also day trading a stock or group of stocks. Swing trading is also possible for serious short-term traders/investors who watch the market closely, but who are not at the trading screen 100 percent of the time that the market is open.

Another kind of short-term position trading is momentum or trend trading. This means that, using your technical analysis, you've identified a particular trend that you believe is emerging, and you execute a trade with the intention of riding that trend until it ends (or comes near the end).

Whatever your style, you must plot your strategy methodically and deliberately. There is no shooting from the hip just because a stock is moving. Every trade, every time must be based on a careful study of the technical factors with confirmation of the trend—or countertrend—found in the intraday dynamics.

7

Stepping through the Trades

There is no better way to learn than by doing—especially if you have someone looking over your shoulder and telling you how you're doing. In this chapter, we're going to step through some recent trades. We've chosen some of my S&P futures trades from the pit, some Nasdaq futures trades from the screen, and some short-term and day trades on individual stocks. My goal is to show you not only what we saw on the chart but also what our thought processes were. Remember, trading is a process with distinct parts from setup through execution. That process may take a split second. But when you break down the steps, you'll see the correlation (or the lack thereof) among what you saw on the screen, your interpretation of the market, and the action you took.

MARCH 21, 2001

As noted in our Morning Meeting at TeachTrade.com on March 21, 2001, the consumer price index (CPI) was released that morning, a touch higher than expectations. Stock index futures had sold off a bit in preopening (the end of the Globex overnight session), and S&Ps made a low on Globex at 1142. When our meeting got underway around 8 A.M. Central time, S&Ps had bounced a bit off the lows at 1147, which was still down 550 points. As part of our commentary, we identified several targets: On the support side we had a key level at 1144.50, then 1142, 1138.50, and 1135. For resistance, we had 1150, 1152, 1158.50 (which was the previous contract low), and 1162. Our technical analysis of the market showed that to get out of immediate danger of further downside S&Ps had to get above 1166.

These were the numbers I had in my head as I walked into the trading pit. I would use these numbers like navigation points for getting short or long, but the activity around me would play a part. Were the big institutions buying or selling? Was there size in this market, or was it just locals trading back and forth?

The opening range was 1150.50 to 1152.50. (See Figure 7.1.) That range encompassed the low from the previous day of 1151, and at this

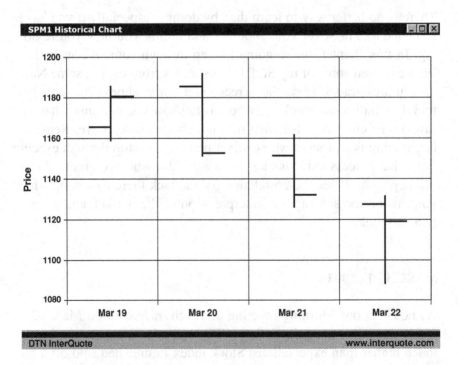

Figure 7.1 SPM1 Historical Chart, March 21, 2001 (*Source:* www.interquote.com, DTN Financial Services)

point the market was above that low. I also knew we had strong resistance at 1158.50, which at that time was the old contract low.

In the first five minutes I scalped back and forth. This means that in the pit I bought and sold a few contracts. At the screen, I probably would have been just watching and waiting. In both cases, however, the setup had not emerged for the move. Then, once the market moved below 1151, which was the previous day's low, I began to trade from the short side, using 1153 as my stop.

I got short—and I stayed short as the market moved lower from 1151. Although I was in the pit, this kind of trade was the same type I would have made at the screen. The setup I was looking for was a decisive move above or below the opening range and the previous day's low. In this case, it was to the downside.

I scaled out of my position at 1145 and 1142. I covered the remainder of the short position at 1139.50, just before the market made a low at 1139.20. My reason for covering there? I knew the market had major support at 1138.50, and if it traded down that low, it could see a significant bounce to the upside.

I always put my exit points about 50 cents above the major support areas because these levels tend to act like magnets—chances are other people will have similar target numbers. (Old highs and old lows are significant on anyone's chart.)

The other thing I saw was that sellers were beginning to retreat as we approached that 1138.50 level. The market looked like it was firming. As I exited the last of my shorts, I shifted to the long side, buying just above the low of the session. When the market rallied back through the level at 1144.50, I covered my position by selling the contracts I just bought. The market kept going, however, for a move of 2,000 points or 20 handles to 1161.

Yes, I missed out on the full extent of the up move. But *nobody* picks the tops and the bottoms on every trade or even most trades. Remember, trade execution is based on your strategy, which in turn is based on your technical levels. If you cover at a previous support level but the market keeps going, then so be it. You trade it the way you see it. You can't yell "Cut!" like some movie director and then start all over again. (And when this market is live, it's like watching a movie—only instead of playing at regular speed, it's as if you're watching on fast-forward.)

I stayed on the sidelines throughout the rally through 1153, 1158.50 and up to 1161. Then, as the buying subsided, I had a very strong bias to the short side. Why? Because of the massive buying we had seen all the way up from 1139.20, I knew that the market had to get above 1166 to be bullish. Remember our Morning Meeting commentary? We said that unless S&Ps could get above 1166, this market was in danger of further downside. Even though there were intraday moves to the upside and the downside, the overall trend was intact. And although this market had rallied 2,000 points, it started stalling at 1160 and then just made it to 1161, sputtering like a car running out of gas.

As the market traded lower and crossed 1158.50, which was the old contract low, and then went up to 1161, I began to initiate short positions. I knew that 1166 would be my ultimate buy stop should this market suddenly gain a head of steam for a big move to the upside. I decided to trade very small, limiting my exposure in case the market turned against me, as I awaited confirmation from the marketplace. Once again, keep in mind that you plot your strategy based on technical analysis, but you wait to see how the market will unfold.

At 1158.50 the market tried to rally, but it failed. When that happened, I increased my short position. As this was an old contract low, I knew 1158.50 would be significant resistance now on the upside. And as we traded below it, the downside was likely to accelerate, probably back to the previous day's lows around the 1151 area.

I covered my short position within the opening range of 1150.50 to 1152.50. When the market failed to hold at the opening range, I went short at 1149.50 to 1149. Note that I didn't just get short at the opening range. I waited to see what the market would do at that very important level. Once it traded below the opening range, that was a signal to me to get short. I scaled out again, first at the support area at 1144.50, then at 1142, and then at 1140. The market made a low of 1137 on that move.

I left the pit in the late morning, as I often do because the market tends to quiet down after 10:30 A.M. Central time until about 1:30 P.M. or so. The best times to trade are those with the most volatility and liquidity. A thin lunchtime trade can chop you up with sudden breaks and rallies that have no follow-through.

In the interim, I reviewed the technical levels. Just as the market is unfolding, so are the technical indicators. A short-term trend line that may be at, say, 1144.50 at the opening will move higher or lower, depending on the range of activity and the market's overall bias.

As of 1:30 P.M. Central time, we were looking for the market to trade above 1146, which was a key area for the afternoon trade. Above that, 1149.50 was another important area, and we were calling for a rally if the market stayed above that level. The market then moved from 1146 to 1153.

Given the overall trend, which still favored the downside, I did not want to trade aggressively from the long side. So as the market traded at 1153, I was looking for an area to get short. I figured I'd place my stop around 1158.50, the area at which the market had tried to rally that morning before failing down to 1137. But the market still looked indecisive to me. As it turned out, it did break down—although I did not have a short position on—and it fell to 1143.

You can't catch every move. In my case, I missed the opportunity to get short. But I didn't want to chase the market. When you're chasing, the odds are too good that you'll end up getting in the market just as it's about to turn and go the other way.

Then, by 2:30 P.M. Central time the market was at 1139.50. In the last 45 minutes of trading things often heat up. If I've been on the sidelines during the early afternoon, I want to be back in the market at 2:30 P.M. There was some buying interest in the pit, enough to tempt a few longs into the market. But the buying quickly dried up. The sellers took over, and the longs had to stampede over each other to get out of their positions.

The key thing to note here was that the range had already been put in during the first two hours of trading, between 1161 and 1139.20. This was the area that was the most heavily traded. We never took out the 1161 high, and the 1158.50 old contract low level was becoming very strong resistance. Add to that the 1151 level, which was the low from the day before and had now turned into a resistance level.

From roughly 2:30 until the end of the session, I was looking for the market to break out of that trading range. Remember, the trend is your friend. In this case the trend was down, so for most of the afternoon I had been trading from the short side.

APRIL 2, 2001

As we've seen on countless occasions, the day of a major economic report the market will be more reactive. In the case of April 2, 2001, the National Association of Purchasing Management (NAPM) report was going to be released around 9 A.M. Central time. Just days before, the Chicago Purchasing Managers index (see Resources), a precursor to NAPM, had come in with the lowest reading since 1982. As we stated in the Morning Meeting, if something were to happen on the national front, the odds increased dramatically that the Federal Reserve would cut rates before the next Federal Open Market Committee (FOMC) meeting.

In the preopening, S&Ps were roughly unchanged at 1169.30. Our upside resistance targets were 1170, 1173.50, a key level 1176.50, and then a cluster between 1179.50 and 1180.50. If we got over this level, then 1181 to 1182 would be the objective, and a strong indication for the upside. On the downside, we outlined a key area at 1167.50 and then a major area at 1166.50, followed by 1164.50, 1162.50, and 1159.50. Further, we had indicator lines at 1165 and 1168 that would tend to act as pivotal areas; above them, the market favors the long side and below them the short side.

My bias at the start of the trading day was toward the short side. We opened at 1168, right on one of the indicator lines. (See Figure 7.2.) I went short around 1168.50, believing that the market would not be able to gain momentum above this level. But buying came into the market, and I was stopped out of my position around 1174.50.

What had happened at this point was the market had shown initial strength all morning. But then we reached our first key resistance area at 1176.50. From 1176.50 through the high of 1179, sellers came into this market, including brokers handling volume.

I had a short bias for the day, even though the market had moved

Figure 7.2   SPM1 3-Minute Chart, April 2, 2001 (*Source:* www.dtnfs.com, DTN Financial Services)

against me earlier with a losing trade from the opening. The session high of 1179 was just below a resistance cluster at 1179.50 to 1180.50. The next level was a major upside objective at 1181 to 1182, which would prove to be strong resistance.

When the market couldn't get through the resistance cluster or even approach the upside objective, I started selling again, getting short between 1176.50 and 1178.50 (below the resistance cluster that began at 1179.50). The market broke down to the 1174.50 area, which was where my stop was on the first trade. I started covering my short position there.

When the market broke under 1174.50, I started getting short again, expecting the market to return to the 1168 level at which we had opened. As we approached 1168, I covered part of my short position.

At that point, I sold 1168—then immediately stopped myself out of the trade with a scratch (no win, no loss). I didn't want to get short there. It was right at the opening range, which often acts as a pivot. At this level, it was a 50–50 trade, which are not good odds for making a low-risk, high-probability trade. Instead, I waited to see what the market would do.

More buying came in, and the market climbed a bit higher; then the sellers returned in force. That was where I got short for a profitable trade.

One of the lessons to take away from this series of trades was my decision to use 1168 as a kind of pivot. That means at this level the market could go either way. That's why I exited that short position at 1168 immediately; it would have been a 50–50 trade. Even if in hindsight it would have ended up being a profitable trade, it was far better for me to keep my discipline and wait on the sidelines until a trading signal was confirmed.

APRIL 26, 2001

Nasdaq futures were up sharply on the Globex overnight session, trading 1,600 points higher at 1840. (See Figure 7.3.) This was an impressive preopening given the fact that Qualcomm (at that time the third

---

Legends, Language, and Lore of Traders

Dead cats don't bounce . . . much. First, our apologies to all the cat lovers out there. We didn't name this move. It's just called the "dead cat bounce."

Everyone knows that when a live cat jumps from a height it will land on its feet and take off. A dead cat won't. If a dead cat were to be dropped from a height it may bounce a little, but it won't move. (Now, don't go trying this on any cats, living or dead.)

It's the same thing with a "dead cat bounce" in the market. The market breaks, hits a support level and bounces a little, and then . . . nothing. It doesn't move. It's a dead cat bounce.

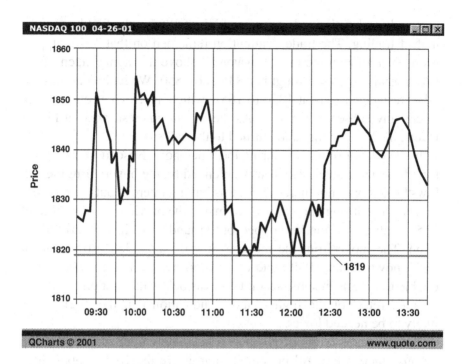

Figure 7.3   Nasdaq Futures Chart (*Source:* www.interquote.com, DTN Financial Services)

largest component in the Nasdaq 100) had issued a statement lowering guidance sharply going forward.

In our Morning Meeting commentary, we had outlined resistance between 1845 and 1855. If this market were to get above that, the next major upside target was 1880. On the downside, we had support between 1820 and 1810. In fact, there had been strong support around the 1819 level, which was heavily defended by the buyers. Below that, we looked for a move to 1790, with limit down coming in at 1782.

On the afternoon of April 25, traders saw strong support around the 1819 level, which was heavily defended by the buyers. Each time Nasdaq futures traded to that level, the market quickly bounced off and went higher. That 1819 level became a support trend line to guide trading decisions for the next day, Thursday, April 26.

The market gapped open substantially higher at 1854 and after pulling back briefly made a session high of 1857 in the first hour and a half of trading. The traders' attention remained on that 1819 support level, even though the market was well above it, trading much of the late morning between roughly 1835 and 1850. We had identified another resistance zone at 1850 to 1855, which appeared strong enough to cap any subsequent moves. As the buying interest faded at higher levels, the bias for this trade turned to the sell side.

In the late morning and during the lunch hour, Nasdaq futures again tested the 1819 level, which was defended by the buyers. But the follow-through was not there. There was buying interest, but the momentum was not strong enough even to match the previous session high of 1857. Rather, the market topped out around 1848 in the early afternoon. The move from the morning low of about 1825 to a high of 1857, down to near 1840, and up to 1850 had formed a classic M or double top. And since the second top was below the first one, this was a failed retest of the highs—and a indication that the market was likely to be headed lower.

But the traders did not go short immediately after that second top because there were still buyers present above the 1819 support line. With one selling signal already generated—the failed retest of the highs—the traders watched for what the market would do when it hit the 1819 support line.

Around 2:15 to 2:30 P.M. Central—a time that activity typically picks up in the market—Nasdaq futures broke through the 1819 support level. With this second, strong sell signal, the traders got short at 1818 and rode short positions all the way down to 1785. The 1785 level was the low before the initial breakout to the upside on the previous day.

Patience and constant monitoring of the trend lines paid off for a well-executed short trade.

MAY 9, 2001

As you'll read in the next chapter, Cisco Systems (CSCO) is one of the Big Five stocks that my partner, Brad Sullivan, and the junior traders at our firm watch as part of their analysis of the Nasdaq futures market. On May 8, 2001, Nasdaq futures had seen a strong opening at 1948 on news that an analyst had issued upgrades. Nasdaq futures had set a high of 1949 on May 8, then traded to a low of 1894, before closing at 1942.50.

In our Morning Meeting for May 9 (see Figure 7.4), we noted that Nasdaq futures were trading limit down at 1950 at the end of the overnight Globex session. We outlined support between 1890 and 1885 and then 1875 to 1865. A very strong band of support was between 1850 and 1835. On the upside, we saw resistance between 1900 and 1910, and then another band of resistance at 1925 to 1935, which could prove tough to get through. The ultimate upside target, if things really got moving higher, was 1960, which was the previous Monday's high.

The overall tone of the market, however, was one of anticipation. The trading range was tight, and explosive moves to the upside or

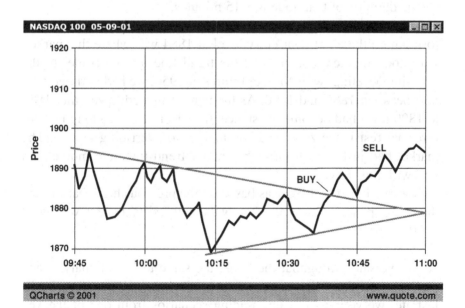

Figure 7.4 COMPX Historical Chart (Nasdaq Composite Index—Combine) (*Source:* www.interquote.com, DTN Financial Services)

downside appeared unlikely. Volume had been paltry. The reason? The producer price index (PPI) report was coming out on Friday, and the Fed was meeting the next Tuesday.

Nasdaq futures gapped lower at the opening to 1900.50. It was a low-volatility morning trading session, with lower highs and higher lows that created a wedge pattern. As discussed in Chapter 4, wedge patterns indicate a tightening range, which the market will break out of eventually. The question was, in what direction?

We drew trend lines on our chart, connecting the previous highs and the previous lows. Extending them out into the future, we formed the apex of the triangle. About three-quarters through that triangle pattern, we knew, a breakout was likely to occur.

The market broke above the resistance line (the top line of the triangle) around 1884. There was good momentum on this upward move, and we went long Nasdaq futures at 1884, with an exit target around 1895, which was the previous high from which we had drawn the triangle.

The duration of that trade was 15 minutes.

To recap, the setup on the trade was based on the wedge pattern forming on the chart. Our entry level at 1884 was where the market, with good momentum, violated the trend line to the upside. In the Morning Meeting, with Nasdaq futures at 1950, we had outlined support between 1885 and 1890. As the market moved lower, that 1885 to 1890 level had become resistance. Our decision to go long just before that resistance zone was due mainly to overriding factors. The market had just broken through a major trend line, and momentum was with this move.

Our exit target of 1895 was based on the previous high that formed the wedge pattern. It was also below the key resistance area we saw at 1900 to 1910.

As we've said throughout the book, the same technical analysis and trading strategies will work regardless of what you're trading. To illustrate, we've chosen a few trading scenarios from one of the key Nasdaq stocks that we track, in this case Ciena Corporation (CIEN).

Like much of the tech sector, Ciena has seen a pretty wild ride. Its 52-week range (as of May 9, 2001) was $151 to $33.50. Ciena is among the stocks in the Nasdaq second tier that we watch as an indicator of what the Nasdaq 100 is likely to do.

It's clear to see from Figure 7.5 Ciena was in a downtrend for most of March. On March 7, 2001, Ciena traded to an intraday high of $78.25, and settled at $75.3125. It declined steeply, settling on March 12 at $53.3125. It traded mostly in the low $50s then rallied briefly, settling at $58.625 on March 22.

Connecting the highs at $78.25 and $58.625 would produce a trend line that this stock would have to trade above to gain any upside momentum. Our patience watching this stock was rewarded. Ciena did break out to the upside, crossing the trend line on April 11. On that

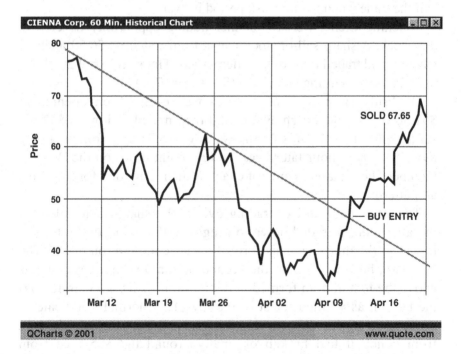

Figure 7.5 CIEN Historical Chart (Ciena Corporation) (*Source:* www.interquote.com, DTN Financial Services)

day, Ciena opened at $51.10, traded as high as $52.75, and closed at $48.93, above the trend line. As buyers above $48, we had an exit target at $58. That was a significant high made in late March, before a sharp break into the mid-$30s, and would pose significant resistance on the next uptrend.

On April 18, Ciena reached and surpassed our target. The stock opened at $59.36, and traded as high as $67 and as low as $57.35 before settling right on our target at $58.06.

What happened then? Ciena did trade as high as $70.89 on April 20, but we had picked $58 as our exit target because of the trend line guiding our decisions and the previous highs at $58. So even though the market might continue higher, the risk of hanging on to a short-term position beyond $58 would have exceeded our risk parameters. Bear in mind that you want to enter a trade when the risk is low and exit the trade when the low-risk period is over.

Watching Ciena, we saw another trading opportunity develop in this stock. A sharp sell-off took Ciena from roughly $56.50 a share, where it had traded most of the afternoon of Thursday, April 26, down to $52 a share, settling at $52.15. (See Figure 7.6.)

On Friday morning, the stock moved even lower, opening at $51.50. It traded as high as $52 and then traded as low as $47.85. As the chart reveals, this first move down to $47.85, followed by a move to $48 an hour later, was the first point down on the W. (Remember, these patterns are not exact. Rather, you look for the overall pattern.)

The stock then rallied, trading over $50 a share, then failed. In the afternoon, it traded down to roughly $48.50, but did not go as low as in the morning. This formed the second point on the W. The key here, however, is that the second bottom in the afternoon was above the first bottom formed in the morning. This is a classic double bottom as a failed retest of the low. That normally indicates a move to the upside. We saw this as a low-risk trade to retest the area from which it had broken originally around the $55 area from Thursday afternoon.

Our buy signal was generated at $49 to $50, following the retest of the lows, on good volume that took the market higher. On Friday, the

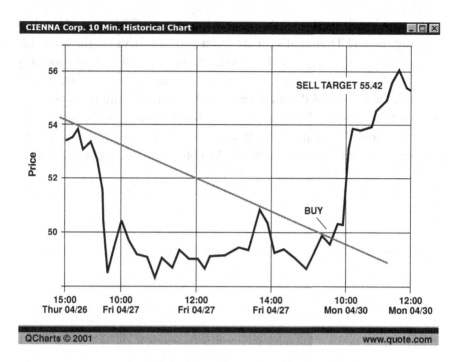

Figure 7.6 CIEN Historical Chart (Ciena Corporation) (*Source:* www.interquote.com, DTN Financial Services)

market closed at $50.29. On Monday, April 30, Cien opened at $53.50, made a low of $52.47, then continued steadily higher to settle at our target of $55.06.

As you become proficient with trading, your decision making will be influenced by the patterns you see repeated over and over, as well as how the market behaved before, during, and after the formation of those patterns. That will become part of your own "inner log" of trades.

And speaking of trading logs, it is very important for you to keep a log of every trade that you make. This will give you a record of what you've done each day, which over time will help you to analyze your strengths and weaknesses. For example, as you look at two weeks' worth of intraday trades (or short-term trades spanning a longer time frame) what do you see? Are you more successful buying dips than selling rallies? Then that's an area you want to focus on for improvement. How long are you holding your winners? How long do you stay in your losers? If you are hanging on to losing trades too long, you'll want to hone your skill and discipline for exiting losing positions.

Also, what time of day do you have the best success? When do you do the worst? This will also help you to know when you're likely to be the most productive in the market. As you trade, the market will teach you—if you're willing to be a student.

8

Trading the Nasdaq

Just say the word "Nasdaq" and what images come to mind? In 1999 the image would have been a highflier of the F-18 variety, zooming skyward. The Nasdaq Composite ended 1999 with a jaw-dropping 85.59 percent gain over the previous year. Dot-com was king; technology was the key to the present and the future.

Then came 2000. It's as if the collective investing public forgot some of the most basic, fundamental lessons—things like "What goes up must come down," "Trees don't grow to the sky," and "Where there is the potential for high returns, there is also a commensurate higher risk."

In 2000, with Nasdaq price/equity ratios at inflated, triple-digit levels, reality began to set in. By the end of that year, the Nasdaq Composite was off 39.29 percent. The downturn continued into the first quarter of 2001, as phrases like "tech wreck" became household terms. As of the end of the first quarter of 2001, the Nasdaq Composite was off 25.1 percent versus the fourth quarter of 2000, and was 59.80 percent lower than the first quarter of 2000.

That highflier, it appears, crashed-landed.

There are several reasons for this decline, from the bursting of the dot-com bubble to nervousness in the economy in general and the tech sector specifically. One thing that can't be overlooked, however, is the very nature of this index and of its recent performance. A high-volatility stock or index will have wild gyrations. The issue for the Nasdaq, technically speaking, is that this spike up, spike down action over the past two years means it could very well have some tough going ahead of it. Nervous investors who were burned—some to the tune of tens of thousands of dollars in margin calls on ill-fated Nasdaq stocks—have not been eager to jump back into this market. Therefore, it's no surprise that this market is expending a lot of energy trying to gain footing to the upside, and would probably experience a lot of slips backward. In the meantime, amid recession fears and despite some aggressive action by the Federal Reserve, the Nasdaq is still (as of this writing in April 2001) below the 3000 level, and the 5000 level is but a distant memory.

Does that mean that everyone will abandon the Nasdaq as an index or any stock that has at least four letters in its symbol (which connotes a Nasdaq issue)? Of course not. But the overall dynamics of the Nasdaq market must be considered before entering this market or continuing to trade it.

In this chapter, we'll look at some key issues. Among them:

- Watching key stocks in the index to help determine the sentiment and future direction of this index.

- Using subindexes, such as the Semiconductor index (SOX) as a proxy to help you gauge what the broader Nasdaq might do on a given day.

- How the Nasdaq affects the other two major indexes—the S&P and the Dow.

The Nasdaq futures are based on the value of the Nasdaq 100 index (NDX), which represents the largest and most active nonfinancial domestic and international issues listed on the Nasdaq, based on market capitalization. The Nasdaq reviews the composition of the 100 index on a quarterly basis, adjusting the weightings of the index components. For example, as of April 25, 2001, the five biggest stocks in the Nasdaq 100 and their weightings were:

1. Microsoft (MSFT)—10.37 percent

2. Intel (INTC)—5.74 percent

3. Qualcomm (QCOM)—4.52 percent

4. Cisco Systems (CSCO)—3.49 percent

5. Oracle (ORCL)—3.3 percent

(To view the Nasdaq 100 and its components, see the Nasdaq/American Stock Exchange web site at www.amex.com and click on Market Activity to view the market indexes.)

Another well-known Nasdaq index is the Nasdaq Composite, which measures all Nasdaq domestic and non-U.S.-based common stocks listed on this exchange. This index is market value weighted, meaning that each company affects the index in proportion to its market value, which is calculated by multiplying total shares outstanding by the last sale price. Thus, the biggest guns in this index—the stocks with the highest share prices and the most outstanding shares—carry the most weight. Currently, there are more than 5,000 companies in the Nasdaq Composite, making it larger than the other major stock indexes. (The Dow Jones Industrial Average is based on 30 stocks, and the S&P 500 is—as the name implies—based on 500 stocks.)

The Nasdaq futures are very volatile, reflecting the gyrations of the component stocks that dominate this index. Nasdaq futures, for example, have about three-times greater volatility than S&P futures. In other words, on the basis of volatility alone—not on contract value— one Nasdaq futures contract would be equivalent to trading three S&P futures.

ROCKET RIDE . . .

What's it like to experience that kind of volatility as a trader? If the S&P contract was a jet, the Nasdaq would be a rocket. The Nasdaq changes direction quickly, without losing speed. Therefore, the Nasdaq can have bigger and quicker moves. That sometimes means a greater chance for a profit (since traders live by volatility). But that also means that the fake-outs can be more dramatic, and the rally that you've been counting on can fizzle as quickly as it materialized. Still, the volatility of the Nasdaq market accounts for the general appeal of trading this market.

At TeachTrade.com we post intraday comments on stock index futures, following the movements of S&P futures and Nasdaq futures. Nasdaq 100 futures, based on the value of the underlying Nasdaq 100 index, are traded in the pit and electronically at the Chicago Mercantile Exchange. At TeachTrade, the Nasdaq futures market is monitored and analyzed by my partner, Brad Sullivan, a very gifted and experienced trader, and a team of junior traders who work with him.

A former stock trader, Brad uses certain key equities as indicators of what the Nasdaq is likely to do—and vice versa. His ability to read the market from a variety of perspectives is one of the hallmarks of his success. He also embodies the kind of discipline and focus that make for a successful trader. Brad is 100 percent a screen trader. Standing six-foot-six, he was an imposing figure during a brief stint in the trading pit where size does bring a certain advantage. If you are head and shoulders above the crowd—literally in Brad's case—it's easier to spot you when you're looking to make a trade. But after a brief foray on the floor at the Merc, mainly to experience what that trading venue is like before the marketplace becomes increasingly electronic, Brad makes his living at the screen where he can more easily monitor multiple markets, guide and monitor the activity of the junior traders in the market, and post commentary intraday on the TeachTrade.com web site.

As Brad explains, to trade the Nasdaq futures, you must watch the action of the "big five"—the top five holdings in the Nasdaq 100, which at this writing are Microsoft, Intel, Qualcomm, Cisco, and Oracle. Together, these five stocks equate to more than 25 percent of the entire index's capitalization. Put another way, what happens to these five stocks is going to have the most significant impact on the overall index. Therefore, it only stands to reason that you must understand and know the movements of at least these stocks on a daily basis.

Take one of Brad's TeachTrade comments (posted live on the web site the afternoon of Friday, February 9, 2001. "We have support in CSCO [Cisco] between 28.50 and 28 dating back to 1999. If we fail and close below, it targets a move toward 22, which should take the NDX with it."

Dissecting this comment, what we're saying here is if the price of Cisco were to fall below $28 for the first time since 1999, this stock would likely be headed toward $22 a share.

There are numerous examples from recent Nasdaq history of the impact one stock can have on the overall index. Let's take an example from more recent history: After the close on April 17, 2001, Intel reported first-quarter net income that beat expectations and made upbeat comments about the second half of the year. ("Stocks Expected to Surge Out of the Gate," by Haitham Haddadin, Reuters, April 18, 2001.)

On the strength and optimism of the Intel news, the Nasdaq composite, which had closed at 1923 on April 17, opened at 2005 on April 18. That was also the day of the surprise 50-basis-point Fed cut that pumped the market higher, sending the Nasdaq composite to a high of 2129 before settling at 2079. (See Figure 8.1.)

More good news followed, with the anticipation that the bottom would be put in place in second-quarter 2001 and that for the rest of the year the outlook would be less bleak—if not downright rosier. ("Many High-Tech Firms Say Q2 the Bottom for Profits," Reuters, April 20, 2001.)

But when it comes to analyzing the broad market or making an intraday trade, the same caution applies: Never try to pick a top or a bottom. By the time Intel's earnings and outlook were announced and the Fed took its actions, it's as if the market had forgotten all about Cisco, which on April 17 had issued an earnings warning.

DON'T PICK TOPS, BOTTOMS

Clearly, the market has a will and whims of its own. The only way to know the bottom has been put in—on a short-term or longer-term basis—is when the market proves that to you over time. An awful lot of

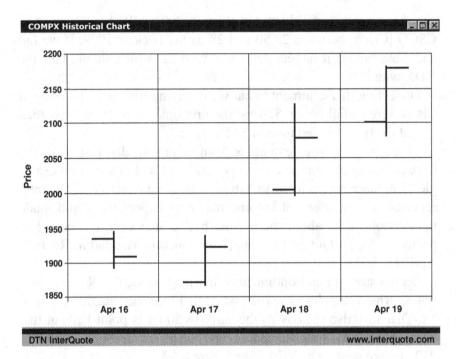

Figure 8.1 COMPX Historical Chart (Nasdaq Composite Index—Combine) (*Source:* www.interquote.com, DTN Financial Services)

people said, "This has to be the bottom," in the first quarter of 2001, only to have the Nasdaq move even lower in April. That's why—and especially in ultravolatile markets like the Nasdaq—it's vital to keep in mind that every day, every trade has dynamics of its own.

As Brad noted in TeachTrade's "Week in Review" for April 21, 2001, the performance of that Intel-Fed week was undeniable. The Nasdaq 100 was up 36 percent from its low earlier in the month, and the bellwether Semiconductor index (SOX) was up nearly 50 percent.

While speculative fever has not quite gripped the market, there has been a perception that the worst is behind us. And while that perception may be true and is something that we've been calling for over the past many weeks, something disturbing has emerged: that is the velocity of this upmove. . . . Certainly one has to wonder and be extremely concerned about the phenomenon that is occurring in the Nasdaq. In spite of the massive decline in individual issues, the valuations have remained extremely high. . . . This leaves us to question how much more upside can there possibly be?

By the time this book comes out, the April move will be part of history, and who knows what market moves will have taken place. We won't venture to make any predictions here, but one thing is certain if you look at the pattern of the past. The Nasdaq, in particular, remains a volatile, trigger-happy market that moves on some earnings reports and warnings, shrugs others off, and has an emotional quality that can seesaw from euphoria to dire pessimism.

If you're going to trade the Nasdaq or Nasdaq stocks, you can't trade in a vacuum. All market forces exert an influence to some varying degree, and possibly in contrary ways. On April 17, for example, Cisco cast a short-term pall on the market, which later shrugged off that news and then skyrocketed on Intel. That's why you must use an integrated approach to trade setup and execution.

STOCKS TO WATCH

When it comes to trading Nasdaq futures, one of the most commonly asked questions is, What stocks are we watching? The answer is, It depends on the day. As outlined earlier in examples, if one of the major stocks—such as Cisco, Intel, or Microsoft—is in the news, it will exert at least a psychological influence on the market, either positive or negative. For follow-through, however, it's important to see what other stocks in that particular sector (biotech, semiconductor, networking, etc.) are also affected. In other words, if a semiconductor stock is impacted by worries about future revenue and earnings growth, is it a company-specific concern or a symptom of the state of the industry?

Looking beyond just an individual stock to what's happening sectorwide is vitally important in a market such as the Nasdaq, which is so dominated by technology. So when you're using stocks to trade an index, one of the keys is to study these equities in much the same way you would the index. In particular, you need to watch the intraday support and resistance levels for these key equities. If one or more of these benchmark equities breaks through critical support to the downside or rallies through key resistance to the upside, you can expect some impact on the index overall. Again, remember that the largest stocks in the index exert the most influence. So when they are impacted, the tremor is felt throughout the index.

There are other benchmarks that act as proxies for the overall behavior of the Nasdaq index. Among them are:

- Semiconductor index (SOX): Traded on the Philadelphia Stock Exchange, this price-weighted index is composed of 16 U.S. companies primarily involved in the design, distribution, manufacture, and sale of semiconductors. The index was set to an initial value of 200 on December 1, 1993, and was split two-for-one on July 24, 1995, according to the exchange.

- PHLX/TheStreet.com Internet Sector (DOT): Also traded on the Philadelphia Stock Exchange, this is an equal-dollar-weighted index composed of 24 leading companies involved in Internet commerce, service, and software. The DOT was set to an initial value of 200 on September 30, 1998.

- Nasdaq Biotechnology index (IXBT). This index contains companies primarily engaged in using biomedical research. Established on November 1, 1993, the Biotech index began trading with a base of 200.

- Amex Networking index (NWX). This index of networking stocks, the largest of which at this writing is Cisco, trades on the American Stock Exchange.

In addition, many Nasdaq players watch—and trade—the QQQs, a tracking stock based on the Nasdaq 100 index. The QQQs are used by both individual and institutional investors to participate in the Nasdaq, but in the form of a tracking stock that seeks to follow the performance of the Nasdaq 100 but at a fraction of the value—(about one-fortieth)—of the underlying index.

In addition to these subindexes, there are individual equities that bear watching. As discussed earlier, there are the big five of Microsoft, Intel, Qualcomm, Cisco, and Oracle. While we keep a sharp eye on these issues, we also closely watch what we call our "second tier." Currently, they include Juniper Networks (JNPR), Ciena Corporation (CIEN), Applied Materials (AMAT), Veritas Software (VRTS), and Checkpoint Software (CHKP).

The movements of the major stocks and the second-tier stocks are like navigation points for charting the probable next direction (or at least giving hints about it) of the broader Nasdaq market. Let's take an example from some of TeachTrade's commentary archives. On February 13, 2001, amid pronounced market weakness, Brad noted intraday, "Now the [second] tiers are just giving back their session [gains]. . . . In addition, the SOX continues to struggle. More importantly, we are now nearing our critical support zone, below which new contract lows are the target." Again, dissecting this comment, the downturn in second-tier stocks and a stall in the SOX signaled trouble ahead for the Nasdaq. At the end of the trading day, the SOX ended the day off 12.40 or 1.9 percent, and the second-tier stocks also settled downward. Nasdaq futures traded down 75.50 points at 2226.

And there are times when Brad will watch a particular technical stock—even though it may not be in the Nasdaq—because its earnings outlook or comments by an analyst on that stock have broader implications for technology stocks in general. For example, EMC Corporation (EMC), a data storage company that trades on the New York Stock Exchange, was on the radar screen on April 11, 2001, when the Nasdaq was under pressure. As Brad wrote in intraday commentary:

What is most important in here is the erosion of confidence. . . . EMC provided the best example of this. While not in the NDX, the analogy is certainly applicable. EMC announced it will miss earnings expectations by 0.02. Instead of selling off, the stock opened unscathed and traded up to 36—nearly $2 higher on the session. But soon the frenzy failed and we went lower. The stock is now on the lows at 32, off 2.34—an apt proxy for the NDM [Nasdaq futures, June contract symbol M].

So how do you know what to watch? If you try to keep track of everything, you'll soon be lost in a sea of information that you're too overloaded to process. Rather, you need to be selectively focused on your radar screen on those stocks and subindexes that have an influence or act as a proxy (meaning what happens to them is an indicator of what's going to happen in the broader market) for the Nasdaq. Here are some suggestions of what a Nasdaq futures trader should be tracking daily and intraday.

- Keep the top five stocks on your screen. Watch for activity at support and resistance levels, retracements, and so forth in these stocks. Keep an ear tuned to the financial news for announcements or comments regarding these stocks. If one of the big five is suddenly upgraded or downgraded by an analyst, or makes a comment about earnings, you can expect the impact to be felt in the Nasdaq 100.

- Watch the second-tier stocks. While their weighting in the Nasdaq 100 is not as large as the big five, they do cast their share of influence over the market. It's particularly important to watch the second tier when the market is discounting (meaning ignoring) the movement in the big five. For example, if one of the big five releases earnings that miss estimates, but that shortfall had already been factored in by the market, then the actual news will have little impact on the trade. Rather, the real sentiment indicator would shift to the second tiers.

- Be on the alert for news in other technology stocks, even if they aren't Nasdaq issues. What happens to IBM has a broader scope of influence than just the S&P 500. IBM is a technology stock, of course, and if news on IBM has ramifications for the technology sector, look for a ripple to go through the Nasdaq.

- Given the dominance of technology on the Nasdaq, watch for movements in the subindexes, such as the SOX (Semiconductors) and DOT (Internet), mentioned earlier in this chapter. The SOX is often a proxy for the Nasdaq. Many times, if we see a rally in the SOX, we can expect the Nasdaq to turn around, and when the SOX breaks Nasdaq is soon to follow.

- If you're trading Nasdaq stocks, your radar screen will look much the same. You'll be tracking the movements of the Nasdaq 100 futures and the subindexes. In addition, keep an eye on similar sectors. For example, if you're trading a networking stock, look at other companies in that sector. If a rally or a sell-off in one stock is not company-specific but rather sector-related, you will want to know that as soon as possible.

- Read the headlines. There are many online news sources that you can scroll through during the day. If you can configure your screen to have scrolling headlines, then do so. Keep the financial news on the television during your trading session. Or go to one of the many online news sites (see Resources) for updates on the market and individual issues.

STOCK WATCHING—HOW IT WORKS

It's important to note that we spend as much time analyzing the top 30 stocks in the Nasdaq 100 as we do the index futures themselves. What we're looking for is a significant movement in one or more of these key stocks as an indication of what might happen in the broader index.

For example, on April 16, 2001, Microsoft closed above its 200-day moving average. (That date was also two days before the Federal Reserve's surprise 50-basis-point rate cut.) Microsoft's crossing of the 200-day moving average was in itself a significant move, given the pressure that this stock and other technology issues had been under. But what could it mean? The important thing is to analyze this kind of information and use it within the proper framework. What the move in Microsoft told us was that the biggest stock in the Nasdaq 100 had crossed a milestone, and because of this it gave us a hint that the rest of the index could be poised for a potential turnaround. (See Figure 8.2.)

VOLATILITY AND STOPS

When it comes to trading the Nasdaq, you have to account for greater volatility in this market. Put another way, you often can't trade Nasdaq futures the same way that you'd trade S&P futures. The intraday range and swings in Nasdaq are usually far wider than in S&P futures. Add to that the volatility of the underlying issues—and the thinness

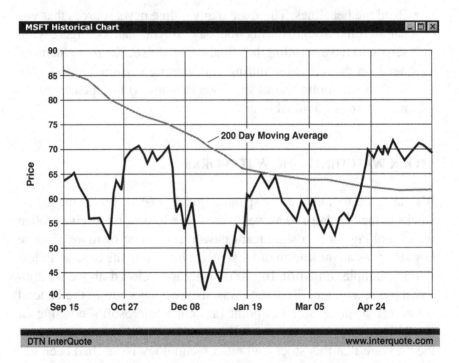

Figure 8.2 MSFT Historical Chart (Microsoft Corporation) (*Source:* www.interquote.com, DTN Financial Services)

(or lack of volume) in Nasdaq futures pit trading—and this makes for a unique market to say the least.

Given these dynamics when it comes to trading the Nasdaq, you must consider your use of stops. As I've said previously in the book, but it bears repeating, never trade without stops. However, there are times of extreme or abnormal volatility when stops should be widened to account for the fact that a market could go against you momentarily and then reverse and go in your direction before you have time to react. If your stops aren't wide enough to accommodate these gyrations, you could get stopped out too soon and miss an opportunity to trade.

Because of the Nasdaq's generally volatile nature, Nasdaq futures require traders to use wider stops than they normally would. Our professional traders, for example, use fairly wide stops as a rule in Nasdaq futures. In general, you might consider stops that take into account a 1.25 percent to 3 percent move. But remember, when you widen your stops to that degree you have effectively increased your risk. You are saying that you won't exit an unprofitable trade unless it makes a substantially larger adverse move. The only way to balance that increase in risk is to cut down your trade size, thus reducing the capital you expose on each trade. By cutting your position size, you can keep your overall risk/reward ratio in balance.

Another thing to keep in mind when trading Nasdaq futures (as opposed to Nasdaq stocks in general) is liquidity. Traders looking to play this market have to understand that there is a general lack of liquidity in Nasdaq futures, which have average daily volume of some 20,000 contracts per session. Add to that relative lack of liquidity the volatility of the index. The stocks in the Nasdaq index include some of the largest-capitalization companies in the country. These issues move quickly, especially compared with their New York Stock Exchange counterparts. One reason is because the Nasdaq is a dealer-based market, while the NYSE is a specialist system aimed at keeping a smooth and orderly market. Another is that the majority of the momentum day traders—those who trade stocks based on momentum to the upside or to the downside—trade Nasdaq stocks. Nasdaq stocks also have the advantage of access provided by electronic communications networks (ECNs), and faster access can increase the volatility.

What that means for the Nasdaq trader is that because this pit-traded futures contract is comparatively illiquid you can end up with a wide bid-ask spread. It's not unusual to call the trading floor for a quote and find that the market is 500 "pit points" wide (or 5.00 on your screen), meaning it's 1980 bid and 1985 offered. If you're trading 10 contracts, that's a $5,000-wide bid-ask spread—which is another reason why you can't trade with your stops too close.

There's another phenomenon that we see in volatile markets such as the Nasdaq. It can show up in virtually any traded market, whether a stock or a stock index, particular when conditions are volatile and movements are fast. This is the "air ball."

Once again, the sports analogy: In basketball, when a player shoots for the hoop but misses—no backboard, no rim, no net—it's called an air ball. The minute the ball leaves a player's hands until it hits the floor it doesn't touch anything but air.

This kind of action can happen frequently in the Nasdaq, where an "air ball" can cover as many as 20 handles and sometimes 30 handles—or even more. What happens then is there is nothing between one price and another but "air"—or more precisely, massive acceleration to the upside or the downside.

For example, on February 13, 2001, Nasdaq was trading at 2312 before a final-hour sell-off that took us down to 2212.

Another day from our trade archives was Thursday, September 21, 2000. In the last half-hour of trading, the Nasdaq rose from 3768 to 3810—or 42.00 points or 42 "handles"—all in seven minutes. Six minutes later, Nasdaq futures were back down to 3769—a drop of 41 handles—and closed at 3765, three points below where they took off. Let's take a closer look at this action: at 2:48 P.M. Central time, Nasdaq futures went from 3780 to 3795 in one minute. That's an air ball. Then at 2:51 P.M., it went from 3799 to 3810—11 handles—in another minute, and another air ball. On the downside, in six minutes, Nasdaq dropped all the way back to 3775—or 35 handles.

What causes "air balls"? Perhaps there is speculation about an event or a rumor that circulates that sends a shiver of panic through the market. Short positions are dumped. Long positions are exited quickly. Whatever the reason, it's apparent that air balls—sudden, rapid, and sometimes unexplained events—are going to happen, especially in a dramatically volatile market like the Nasdaq.

EXTENSIONS

Another feature of a volatile market such as the Nasdaq is "extensions," which are simply percentage changes from various moving averages (see Chapter 3). For example, let's say the 20-day moving average in the Nasdaq is at 2500. If the current price is 2650, that would be a 6 percent upside extension. Plotting these extensions on a graph, you can analyze these correlations, to see when—and where— the market is abnormally extended. (Think of a kid on a swing at the playground. That swing can go out and up just so far before it begins to swing back. And it can swing back just so far before it moves forward again.)

Typically what we find is that a bounce or a reversal is more likely to happen when the Nasdaq trades at more than a 12 percent extension from the 20-day moving average. But in recent history, given the dramatic moves in the Nasdaq, we have seen some monumental extensions. For example, at the highs in March 2000 the Nasdaq Composite was about 58 percent above its 200-day moving average, an abnormally wide extension to the upside. The biggest reading on the downside was at the lows of 2001 when the index was 63 percent below its 200-day moving average.

Once you know that, how do you use this information? For one thing, it helps to determine what is likely to happen next. Trading, in many ways, involves finding when the odds of something happening are high, which increases the probability of success for a trade. For example, let's say that the Nasdaq is extended at a very wide percentage (compared with recent activity) from the 20-day moving average. At that point, the odds are slim that you'd get much more of a long position. (Conversely, if the Nasdaq is extended by a very wide percentage below the 20-day moving average, you'd expect that virtually all of the downside potential has been exhausted.) The strategy at that point would be to look for the best place to cover a position and exit. You probably wouldn't jump on the opposite side, however. For one thing, there is still a chance that the market could extend further to the upside or downside—although the odds of a continued significant move are slim. Rather, you'd wait and look for the market to reverse, the next day or the day after that, to take advantage of the extended conditions—either overbought or oversold.

MARKET DYNAMICS

For the sake of those trading the Nasdaq, we would be remiss if we didn't discuss the dynamics of the futures market—both the Nasdaq major contract that trades in the pit at the Merc, and the scaled-down Nasdaq 100 e-mini, which trades electronically. The Nasdaq major contract does not trade that often in the pit. Liquidity there is comparatively light. In the Nasdaq e-mini, however, there are far more price changes. What this means for you, the individual trader, is that in the Nasdaq e-mini, orders, cancels, fills, and reversals can all be done in seconds. But in the pit, these actions can take 10 or 20 seconds—or maybe even minutes.

As a result, quotes and trades in the pit often are playing catch-up with the e-mini. This sets up an arbitrage opportunity between the Nasdaq major and the Nasdaq e-mini for serious, professional players. Granted, to do this you must have a Globex machine (see Chapter 2), the electronic terminal from the Chicago Mercantile Exchange, to trade directly. And you must have someone in the pit trading the Nasdaq major. This kind of setup allows professionals to trade off the price differentials in the e-mini, which tends to react faster to changes in the underlying stocks, and the major.

One other word on liquidity: When you are trading individual Nasdaq shares, make sure there is enough volume and liquidity in the issues you choose. In the beginning, stick with the household names, when you can be assured of strong volume that will make for a fairly orderly trade (even in volatile conditions). Don't try to trade—particularly on a day-trading basis—low-volume stocks. The participation may not be there to make for predictable movement. And when a comparatively large buy or sell order comes in, the stock may overreact to the point of severely undermining your position.

Meanwhile, there is also an interesting dynamic between the Nasdaq and the S&P, which sets up an intriguing interplay between the two markets. As we've seen—especially in 1999, 2000, and thus far in 2001—there are times when one index will dominate, leading the other upward or downward. At TeachTrade.com we are always watching to see if one of the three major indexes is dominating, if one is dragging down the rest, or if all three are moving in concert one way or the other. We often note that for a rally to be sustainable, it needs the three major indexes—Nasdaq, Dow, and S&P—to be moving together to the upside.

When there is a convergence among the indexes, that convergence often is a function of money flow. Often we've seen in first-quarter 2001 and thus far in second-quarter 2001 money flow into and out of techs. On days that the Nasdaq has rallied, we've seen bargain hunters buying Nasdaq tech issues at fire sale prices, often at the expense of the blue-chip and household names of the Dow. Certainly during the "tech wreck," we saw money flow out of techs and into the safe, more value-oriented Dow stocks. Watching the sectors you can see which stocks are in or out of favor at the moment.

Of course, both the S&P and the Nasdaq are reacting to the price movements of the stocks in their relative cash indexes. But the technology-dominated Nasdaq is the quicker of the two to move and react.

For these reasons, Nasdaq traders need to be acutely aware of the type of market they're in. There are times when volatility is high, and traders need to adjust both their strategies and their executions. At other times, volatility contracts and the market is thin, making for an unproductive and fruitless trade. The important thing is to listen to what the market is telling you, instead of to what the pundits are saying it should do. In the first quarter of 2001, while many of the general investing population were looking for (and hoping and praying for) a bottom, traders got caught looking for a breakout that never happened. Time and time again, we saw the market able to rally only from the lows. At the highs, the trade just died. What did that tell us? The market was tentative as it moved higher, and interest evaporated at the highs. The wishful thinkers could postulate all they wanted. The market had the voice of authority, and it was saying, loudly and clearly, that it was not time for the breakout—yet.

As of this writing, the market pundits are more positive. Commerce Department data that shows growth in the economy—with the gross domestic product (GDP) for the first quarter gaining 2 percent instead of an expected 0.9 percent—has been touted as evidence that the economy is okay and recession is not a concern. (At TeachTrade, we cautioned that this is an economic indicator in the rearview mirror and is not a forward projection of growth.) This underscores the need to trade the market as it's presented to you. Don't trade on expectations, or hopes and wishes. You may want a rally, but unless that materializes in the market and is sustained, you can't play the breakout. You may think the market will pull back significantly, but if volatility declines and Nasdaq is stuck in a tight range you have to trade it as such.

That's why, in any trade but especially in the Nasdaq, you must put emotion and expectation aside. Analyze the market that you're trading; watch the charts and the other indicators. And remember, the Nasdaq is a different kind of animal: fast and unpredictable. Unless you can be quick to analyze moves as they're happening, this is not the market for you. But if you like volatility, then you may have found your trading home.

9

After the Bell

The market is closed. As you turn off the screen and clear away the debris of the trading day, you know where you stand regarding your position (long, short, or "flat" with no position). Throughout the day, you've focused on making well-executed trades and not the money, but now you know where you stand financially. You may feel pumped up by your successes or deflated by your failures. This is the roller coaster that most traders ride, and I'd be lying if I said I wasn't among them. Even after years of successful trading, there are still times when I wake up in a cold sweat in the middle of the night and wonder, "Can I do this anymore? Have I lost it?"

Trading is not only about making money. Yes, it is the way I feed, clothe, and house my family and send my kids to college. But the essence of trading is far more than money; it's about competition. You hone your skills to do battle every day in the market. You can never rest on your laurels, no matter how successful you become. This is a profession that will demand the best you can give every day. And at the end of the day, you will know exactly how well you've stood up to that challenge. You'll suffer the instant loss or enjoy the instant gratification. Then you'll clear your mind and get ready for the next day.

This is the routine I've lived for two decades. I've been privileged to work with and learn from some of the best traders imaginable who took the time to train me and explain how things work. I've tried to extend that legacy by training young traders who had the dedication, discipline, and drive. In these chapters, I've tried to give you what I believe are the essential lessons of day trading.

If you take away one thing from this book, let it be the realization that there is no one surefire indicator, or never-fail system. Trading is a process that begins and ends with you: your technical analysis, your discipline, your trade execution, your commitment. All that adds up to how you do on your inevitable learning curve.

As we wrap up *The Day Trader's Course*, I want to address some of the questions and topics that I'm frequently asked at seminars or in reader e-mails. Chances are these are some of the questions you may also have.

"HOME RUN TRADES"

Many young traders hope for the "big win," the kind of trade that gives them a big profit and bragging rights to a great story after the market closes. They are hungry to take those 20 handles in S&P futures or that 15-point move in a stock. They want this so bad they can taste it. The problem is, in their quest for the big one they may be missing a lot of little ones along the way. Or, worse still, they may try to trade the smaller moves as if they were the big break.

To use yet another sports analogy, you can't swing for the fences every time you're at bat. (Keep in mind that the same year that Babe Ruth led the National League in home runs he also led the League in strikeouts.) Rather, you take your pitch, swing as hard as you can, and run as many bases as you can without getting out. In trading, you devise your trading plan every day, you wait for the setup, and then make your trade. You stay with that trade according to the parameters of your plan. You get in and out of the trade based on the price points identified by your technical analysis.

As a beginning trader, in particular, your goal is to make several well-executed trades. The net result of small profits and even smaller losses is a profit. You may not have "the story" to tell at the bar about the five-figure trade you pulled off. But if you stick with your plan, with well-executed trades and discipline above all else, there is little chance that your buddies will be telling a story about you and your five-figure loss that wiped you out of the market.

Yes, I've made some big trades. But over my 20 years in this profession, I've been more "tortoise" than I've been "hare." Slow and steady—methodical and deliberate—does win the proverbial race. The hare that wants to dash toward the big profits will run out of breath—and capital—too quickly.

EXITING TOO SOON

Many beginning traders complain that they get out of a trade "too soon" and, in hindsight, they see the profit they "could have made." Hindsight, as they say, is always 20–20. But when you're in the thick of things, it may be hard to see clearly. First of all, you should know your exit point and your stop-loss level *before* you execute your trade. You get in at A, your target is B, and you set your maximum loss at C. Then you execute the trade.

If it turns out that B was only the middle of the move and the market eventually went to D, then you should examine your setup again in the light of your technical analysis. It could be that you missed the trading signal that indicated a bigger move. Or the market may have surprised you. In either case, keep in mind two things:

1. Trade according to your plan. If your analysis indicates a price at which to exit and the market keeps going after you do so, then congratulate yourself for sticking with your plan. If you think the market has a chance to make a run beyond your initial target, you may want to scale out of the position. Get out of, say, half your position at the first price target, and then scale out of the rest at other price targets.

2. Nobody ever went broke taking a profit. Better to sell too soon than to hang on too long and turn a winner into a loser.

HANGING ON TOO LONG

For every trader who has the problem of "exiting too soon" there appears to be an equal number who "hang on too long." These traders are so worried they'll miss something that they don't take the profits that they have in their hands. Once again, it goes back to the trading plan. Pinpoint your entry, exit, and stop points and stick with them. You may determine—based on technical indicators and market behavior—that the market could make an extended move in your direction. If that's the case, then reduce your position (taking a profit) at the first target and exit the rest at successive targets. If you scale out of a position, however, remember to move your stop to the first profit target. That way, if the market turns against you, the stop will be at your original target.

When you trade, keep in mind the story of the goose that laid the golden egg. The goose laid only one golden egg per day. Eager to get more all at once, the farmer killed the goose and looked inside. No more golden eggs; just a bloody mess. If a well-executed trade yielded a profit, that's great. But don't hang on to squeeze more of a profit out. If you do, you could end up like that farmer—or the goose.

PRICE TARGETS

Do support and resistance levels become targets for the trade? The answer is yes . . . and no. Remember Chapters 3 and 4 in which we put the first indicators on the chart. When you have a trend line above the market (resistance) and a trend line below the market (support) you have determined the expected boundaries for that market. The only time the market would extend beyond these levels is if it were breaking out in one direction or the other.

Thus, support and resistance act as the initial parameters to define the trade. Beyond the first levels above and below the market, there will be other resistance and support levels. For example (taking an excerpt from our Morning Meeting of May 3, 2001), we identified a support zone between 1262.50 and 1257. Below 1257, we saw another support level at 1248. On the resistance side, we targeted 1264 to 1265 and then 1271. S&Ps opened at 1262 and made a high at 1262.50 (at the end of our support zone) before trading lower to around the 1248 level. Our resistance levels of 1264 to 1265 and 1271 weren't touched. At midday, they continued to define the expected upper parameters of the move. At the same time, it's easy to see that the support levels outlined earlier did act as targets.

You may find that the support and resistance areas that you identify in your technical research are similar to others that you read about in market commentary, such as on TeachTrade.com. Some of this is obvious. If 1270 is a double top, then much of the market focus is going to be on that level. Other aspects are more subtle, such as retracements of particular moves or the observation of two-sided trades (with buyers and sellers both active).

Most importantly, understand that there is really nothing magical about support and resistance areas. They are guides to help you plot your course of trading. The market may reach them; it may not. But knowing where these parameters are will help you to determine where you want to enter and exit your trades.

Identifying the significant support and resistance areas will help you to plot your trade; then, depending on your trading style and time frame, you will trade between those price targets.

S&P FUTURES TRADING

I'm often asked why I trade mostly S&P futures instead of day trading stocks. When it comes to stocks, I make some short-term trades (based on technical analysis) as well as longer-term investments. But I make my living trading S&Ps. Your choice of what you trade is like many life choices. You end up being affiliated with what's familiar to you, and what suits your nature and your personality.

For me, my introduction to trading was in the futures market, at the Merc where I was a runner (the lowest of entry-level jobs), then a clerk, an assistant broker, a broker, and finally an independent trader. The first market I traded was gold—back in the early 1980s when gold was at $800-plus an ounce—and then I moved to S&Ps soon after that pit opened up. I've also traded currency futures and Eurodollar futures. Clearly, my trading career was built on my early experience at the Merc and my affinity for the futures market. I thrived on the volatility and chaos, discovering that when the world around me went crazy I was able to keep sane.

Had my trading career begun differently—as an apprentice to a stock or options trader—I might have ended up trading stocks or options. But S&P futures and I are well suited to each other. To me, this was the ultimate competitive arena, the world's largest stock index futures contract. And anyone who trades anything certainly knows that S&P futures have been an untamable market.

Also, there is the breadth of the S&P market. Institutions come here to lay off portfolio risk, making for good trading opportunities for locals like me. This translates into good trading opportunities, too, for the screen-based traders of both the S&P major and the scaled-down e-mini.

As I've said in Chapter 2, trading the S&Ps also allows me to participate in the broader dynamics of the market, instead of just one or a handful of stocks. Add to that the ability to go short without an uptick (as is required in stocks) and the leverage, margin, and taxation treatment, and I believe that there are some inherent advantages in trading futures.

What you trade will depend on what suits you. You may trade stocks 100 percent of the time, using the movement of the stock index futures as a guide for your trading decisions. You may trade both stocks and futures, depending on the dynamics of the day.

Whatever you trade, the fundamentals are the same. Focus on a liquid market. You don't want to trade a thin stock that's hard to get into or out of. Always use technical analysis to determine entry, exit, and stop points. And remember that trading without discipline is like driving with a blindfold. You're almost certain to crash.

TRADING IN THE PIT

For some 20 years, I've traded on the floor of the Chicago Mercantile Exchange. While the evolution to an electronic marketplace is inevitable, I do believe that open-outcry (yelling out bids and offers in the pit, auction style) will not disappear immediately. Some markets will more easily become all-electronic—such as currency futures—especially if trades tend to be done between brokers, going from order filler to order filler. If local participation is a strong feature, such as in S&P futures, I believe that the pit and the electronic market will somehow coexist.

Readers of this book, however, will 99.9 percent most certainly be screen traders. The closest they come to the pit may be the visitors' gallery at the Merc or another exchange, or perhaps a "squawk box" that broadcasts the activity from the trading floor (much like radio announcers give the play-by-play on the ball game). Still, there remains a fascination for the pit.

For screen-based traders, a visit to the pit is like looking behind the scenes at the filming of a movie. At the screen, you see the action as it is displayed in a dynamic but linear fashion, one tick after another. In the pit, you see what transpired to make that tick. You hear the bids; you hear the offers. You watch the hand signals and gestures as traders make trades with each other.

To the outsider it looks like pandemonium. To the trader in the pit, however, it's an orderly marketplace with nearly instant oversight. If a price is questioned, the pit is immediately notified by an exchange employee who makes an announcement, and if the price is taken out, we know that, too.

But there is no denying that pit trading is like nothing else. There are days when it feels like you're transacting business in a crowded elevator, stuck between floors. On other days, you're standing around, waiting for something to happen.

The differences between pit and screen trading go beyond the physical locales. In the pit, it's possible to make small, quick scalping trades when large orders come into the pit. Some of those trades may last less than a minute. Just by being in the pit, you will be presented with opportunities to buy and sell—to get in and out of positions— quickly, as the market moves. This kind of scalping may be in addition to position trades that you're making, based on your bias and analysis.

At the screen it's virtually impossible to scalp, with the possible exception of when the market is very volatile. On those occasions, you may be able to get into and out of a trade very quickly because of the opportunity that you saw in the market. But in general, screen-based trades—even a quick entry and exit—tend to be more deliberate. You see a potential trade develop on the screen, and you make it. That trade may last minutes or hours.

The computer screen has made another difference in trading: It has eliminated the physical advantage in the pit. Bigger is better in the pit, where to be seen and heard is essential. The trading pit tends to be mostly male and mostly young. At 44, I am an "old" trader in the pit. The physical stamina to stand in that pit for hours a day is a younger man's game.

The screen, however, is the great equalizer. Whether you're the size of a linebacker or a ballerina, it doesn't make any difference. Male or female, young or old, the screen has no preference. Rather, what remains the same is the dedication to the market and the discipline to trade.

There's one more thing that may be helpful. In the pit, you are watching the action with your eyes and hearing the bid/offer action (and the accompanying frenzy of noise). At the screen, as you watch the action, you have to learn to "listen with your eyes" for what the market is telling you.

THE BIGGEST MISTAKE

People sometimes ask me what's the biggest mistake I've ever made. Maybe they've heard the story of how I made $1.3 million in one half-minute trade on the Thursday after the crash of 1987. They want to know if I've suffered a one-trade loss as big. Thankfully, that's not the case. But I've had my share of big losers, too.

Still, those losers aren't the worst mistakes I've ever made. In trading, losses happen. They are inevitable. If you trade big size, you'll stand to increase both your profit potential *and* your loss potential. That's why you never trade bigger than your capital allows. (And remembering the 2:1 reward-to-risk ratio rule, you want to stand to make a minimum of $2 for every $1 that you could lose.)

The biggest mistake anyone could make is believing that they've beaten the market. Nobody beats the market, and I mean nobody. Traders may outperform a particular index. For example, money managers may say they have outpaced the performance of the S&P 500. But have they beaten the market? Have I on my best day of trading? Absolutely not.

Trading successes are the product of being in sync with the market. Your technical analysis, your trade execution, and the movement of the market are aligned. It's what professional athletes call being in "the zone." You find yourself buying at the low and selling at the high. You get in and out of trades that are executed with textbook precision.

But don't ever let yourself be lulled into the feeling that you've mastered the market. Because you can't be in sync with the market every day. There will be some days when you'll have to keep your wits about you as the market gyrates, swirls, and chops its way higher and lower. Focus on making well-executed trades (I know, this sounds like a broken record). Trade what the market is dishing out. Don't look for something that isn't there. And never, ever let yourself believe you've beaten the market.

PAPER TRADING

Take a kid to an arcade some day and let him or her play a racing game. Gripping the steering wheel, the kid stares at a screen that simulates the racetrack. The sound of engines roaring and squealing brakes makes it seem real. But it's only make-believe.

It's much the same with paper trading. It may have the look, feel, and sound of the real thing, but it's only make-believe. However, unlike the arcade game, paper trading can be educational. With paper trading, you can determine where you'd get in and get out of a trade, and where you'd put your stop. Then as the market unfolds, you can see how you did.

But there are two drawbacks to paper trading. One is the temptation to paper trade based on what you *would have* done. For example, you see the break and tell yourself you would have gone short there, covered at a lower price, gone long on the reversal, and taken a profit at a certain point. That's not paper trading. That's basically going over the day's action.

Paper trading is writing down your entry point and your stop during a live market session. If you exit, you mark down that price. If you get stopped out, you write that down, too. At the end of the session, you examine every trade—the winners as well as the losers. Don't gloss over the "dumb moves" because you'd "never do that again." To have any validity as an education tool, every paper trade you put down must be considered. More importantly, that so-called "dumb move" holds a very important lesson for you: the kind of error you may be prone to make when you're trading for real.

That brings up the other drawback of paper trading. There is no money on the line; therefore, it's very difficult to replicate the emotion you will feel when you're trading live. You can't know how you'll act when you have placed a trade until you do. You may have the mechanics down—entering orders, determining your stop, and so on. As stated earlier in the book, when you paper trade, your focus is on the entry and on the exit. There is no emotion tied to every tick along the way—as there is in live trading. Until you put your money down, you won't know how you'll cope with profits and with losses.

Will you become the proverbial deer in the headlights? Will you throw away all your discipline and trade like you're on a suicide mission? You won't know until you have money on the line.

SINGLE-STOCK FUTURES

The creation of financial futures changed the nature of traditional commodity trading. The agricultural contracts—from pork bellies to cattle—that are traded at the Chicago Merc (and the grain futures traded at the Chicago Board of Trade) were certainly the granddaddies of the futures industry. But the financial futures were the new generation. Currency futures had been around at the Merc since the 1970s, and Eurodollar futures (based on the amount of U.S. dollars on deposit overseas) were introduced in 1981.

But the S&P futures contract—based on the value of the Standard & Poor's 500 stock index—was another animal. Here was the benchmark of Wall Street—the S&P 500—used by institutions and portfolio managers. Today, there is a host of financial futures products traded by institutions and individuals alike. They include S&P and Nasdaq majors, S&P and Nasdaq e-minis, Dow futures (on the Chicago Board of Trade), the Nasdaq 100 tracking stock (QQQ) on the American Stock Exchange (Amex), and a variety of sector indexes from biotechnology to banking.

Looking back, we can easily see that the financial markets are continuing to evolve. As long as a need and an interest are perceived, new financial products will be launched. As long as hedgers will use a product to reduce their risk exposure and speculators are willing to participate and provide liquidity, then there will be new markets on the horizon.

The one I'm watching closely is the advent of futures on individual stocks. To me, this has the potential of revolutionizing the markets. But revolutions are often very messy and potentially disruptive.

Single-stock futures will give equity traders another venue to speculate in the movement of particular issues. Plus, futures traders, who already participate in the broader indexes, will be able to speculate in the movement of individual issues. Of course, as with every significant market, there will be the obstacles to overcome. One is regulatory, as in who is going to watch over these futures on stocks? Futures are the purview of the Commodity Futures Trading Commission (CFTC). But stocks come under the watchful eye of the Securities and Exchange Commission (SEC). There is little use in debating here what agency should watch over these futures on stocks. Rather, our attention must be focused on what this means to the marketplace.

Single-stock futures will be a reality. Presumably, by the time this book goes to press, institutions will already be trading futures on stocks. By the end of 2001, individuals are expected to be able to trade them as well. As of this writing, however, it is still uncertain just how and where they will trade. But trade they will. In December 2000, Congress passed the Commodity Futures Modernization Act of 2000, which lifted a nearly 20-year ban on futures based on individual stocks. The reason for this legislative action was to make U.S. exchanges more competitive with overseas markets in places like London and Australia, where futures on individual U.S. equities are already listed.

Now that single-stock futures will be able to trade in the United States, what kind of marketplace will evolve? It appears that these products will require a hybrid approach that brings together two or more exchanges. As of this writing, Chicago's three major futures and options exchanges have said they will jointly form a market in which to trade single-stock futures. This alliance brings together the Chicago Board Options Exchange (CBOE), which will have a 45 percent stake; the Chicago Mercantile Exchange (CME), which will also have a 45 percent stake; and the Chicago Board of Trade (CBOT), which will have a 10 percent stake. The joint venture was targeted to be up and running by August. ("Single-Stock Futures Offer Promise of Fat Profits," by Peter A. McKay and Kopin Tan, *Wall Street Journal*, May 15, 2001.)

Other alliances aimed at listing and trading single-stock futures include a joint venture between the Nasdaq and the London International Financial Futures Exchange (LIFFE). In addition, Eurex, the European all-electronic exchange, may list the single-stock futures in conjunction with the CBOT.

These new products could prove to be very appealing to investors, including those who use options to speculate in stock movements or to hedge equity holdings. As the *Wall Street Journal* article noted:

> The competition among exchanges is expected to be fierce, since the new futures have unique crossover appeal among options, stock and futures markets that rarely compete for the same products. Indeed,

[the May 14] announcement was considered just another in a string of several to come as markets try to tap into one another's expertise to beat other competitors.

"From talking to our customers, they told us they wanted to use single-stock futures to hedge their options positions," CME chairman Scott Gordon was quoted in the article. "Once we heard that, it was pretty clear we should talk to the CBOE."

I believe these will be largely electronically traded futures, allowing for the listing of multiple stocks. In the beginning, probably futures on only the largest stocks will be traded, and by institutions dabbling in them to discover the hedging and arbitrage opportunities.

What should individual traders do? Watch this market to see how it develops. In my opinion, there is certainly a chance that single-stock futures will attract attention (and, eventually, liquidity) because of the margin and leverage advantages inherent in futures, as well as the ability to go short without an uptick. But all markets take time to develop. Just as we saw nearly 20 years ago in S&P futures, a market gains familiarity and then participation. Then when the liquidity is there, other participants will come.

Will we at TeachTrade.com jump into single-stock futures the minute they're launched? No. But will we watch this development closely? Absolutely. And when we determine there is an opportunity to trade, we will trade these products based on our knowledge of equities and our expertise in futures.

Trading any market is learned incrementally. As a trader, you probably start out buying dips. Then you learn to sell rallies. You develop strategies that suit the market's prevailing dynamics. The same process applies to learning a new market. Observe it closely. See how it trades. Then step in, one toe at a time.

WHAT HAPPENS NEXT?

We used to say that for every 10 people who came to the trading floor, 3 out of 10 would make it, and 1 out of 10 would make a good living at it. The rest would either lose all their money, burn out quickly, or decide that the wear and tear on their physical and mental well-being was not worth it.

There is no guarantee I can give anyone that he or she will succeed at trading. What I do know, based on my own experience, is that you can improve your chances of succeeding with a trading plan based on technical analysis and a disciplined approach to trade execution. Beyond that, it is simply a matter of knowing yourself.

Trading is not for everyone, just as law, medicine, teaching, architecture, the arts, professional athletics, or any other occupation isn't for everyone. Trading may interest you. Trading may be your passion. Trading may be your fantasy to make a lot of money and tell your boss to take this job and. . . .

In the least, your foray into trading will be a learning experience, about the market and about yourself. If this is your attitude going in, you won't "lose." You will only stand to win. Don't start out risking more capital than you can afford to lose. If you take the position that you could lose every dime in your trading account and still have your house, your cars, your prized possessions, then you won't be gripped by fear or ruled by greed.

You may find, as I did when I first stepped on that trading floor, that you are at home in the market. It may make sense to you on such a deep level that you couldn't think of doing anything else. You will still have a learning curve ahead of you, and you'll face losses. But, knowing yourself, you will know that you are cut out to trade.

Or you may do well enough, but you may find that trading was not all it was cracked up to be for you. You may find the emotional highs and lows to be more than you want to put up with on a regular basis. Having a day job you enjoy and the security of a paycheck may be far more appealing.

Or you may not do well at all. You may find that, despite all your best efforts, you are not suited for this. Your losses mount. You're losing your confidence, your nerve, and your stomach lining. There is no joy in trading for you.

No matter what the outcome if you approach trading with a desire to learn, then there will be no real loss other than the capital that you could afford to put at risk. The money you lost was simply tuition to attend the University of the Market, which compares with no other place of "higher education." Classes are held almost daily, whenever the market is open. The tuition is the capital you can afford to risk. The syllabus encompasses every facet of market activity and psychological demand you can envision.

The market's open. Now, the real day trader's course begins.

RESOURCES

Economic Calendar

A number of economic reports are released every month that may potentially impact the market. Traders typically analyze these reports for what is now happening economically, as well as a glimpse of what it might mean for the future.

Auto and Truck Sales: Released by automakers from first to third business day of the month. Minimal market impact.

Business Inventories: Released at 8:30 A.M. Eastern time on about the 15th of each month. Compiled by the Department of Commerce. Report includes sales and inventory from manufacturing, wholesale, and retail stages. But much of the data has been released by the time this report is issued. Retail inventory component, however, is watched. Minimal market impact.

Chicago Purchasing Managers: Released at 10:00 A.M. Eastern time on the last business day of the month. One the most closely watched regional manufacturing surveys (along with Philadelphia Fed Index). Compiled with input from purchasing managers and Federal Reserve banks. Often seen as an indicator of the National Association of Purchasing Management (NAPM) report.

Construction Spending: Released at 10:00 A.M. Eastern time on the first business day of the month. Compiled by the Department of Commerce. Report reflects residential, nonresidential, and public expenditures on new construction. Little or no market impact.

Consumer Confidence: Released at 10:00 A.M. Eastern time on the last Tuesday of the month. Compiled by the Conference Board. Based on monthly survey of 5,000 households to ascertain consumer confidence. This report can help predict shifts in consumption patterns. Some market impact.

Consumer Price Index (CPI): Released at 8:30 A.M. Eastern time on about the 13th of the month. Compiled by the Department of Labor. CPI measures prices of a fixed market basket of goods and consumables purchased by consumers. This report has a definite market impact given its role as an inflation indicator.

Durable Goods Orders: Released at 8:30 A.M. Eastern time on about the 26th of the month. Compiled by the Department of Commerce. Measures dollar volume of orders, shipments, and unfilled orders of durable goods (that have an intended life span of three years or more). This report is watched as a leading indicator of manufacturing activity.

Employment Report: Released at 8:30 A.M. Eastern time on the first Friday of the month. This very influential and widely watched report is compiled by the Department of Labor. The Employment Report (which also goes by the names of "Non-Farm Payroll" and the "Unemployment Report") reflects two separate reports that result from two separate surveys. The household survey is of 60,000 households, which is used for the unemployment rate. The establishment survey is of 375,000 businesses, and is used for nonfarm payrolls, average workweek, and average hourly earnings. Potentially large impact on the market.

Existing Home Sales: Released at 10:00 A.M. Eastern time around the 25th of the month. Compiled by the National Association of Realtors. The report reflects sales of existing homes and gives an indication of housing sector activity. Minimal market impact.

Factory Orders: Released at 10:00 A.M. Eastern time around the first business day of the month. Compiled by the Department of Commerce. Consists of earlier announced durable goods plus nondurable goods orders. Little or no market impact.

Federal Open Market Committee (FOMC): The FOMC meetings are widely watched and anticipated. The FOMC has 12 members and holds eight regularly scheduled meetings per year. The role of the FOMC is to direct the lending policies of the Federal Reserve, which in turn governs prevailing interest rates and helps to spur or slow down economic growth. The actions of the FOMC are highly influential on the market. They include rate cuts and rate hikes, statements regarding its bias toward future actions, and virtually any comment regarding the U.S. economy.

Gross Domestic Product (GDP): Released at 8:30 A.M. Eastern time the third or fourth week of the month for prior quarter. Subsequent revisions released in the second and third months of the quarter. Compiled by the Department of Commerce. GDP report is a broad measure of economic activity, including growth rate for total economic output. While this is a backward-looking reading, it is widely watched and can have significant market impact.

Housing Starts/Building Permits: Released at 8:30 A.M. Eastern time around the 16th of the month. Compiled by the Department of Commerce. Housing starts measures the number of residential units for which construction has begun. Market watches this report.

Industrial Production/Capacity Utilization: Released at 9:15 A.M. Eastern time around the 15th of each month. Report compiled by Federal Reserve. Industrial production index measures physical output of U.S. factories, mines, and utilities. Capacity utilization gives some indication of economic strength, since it measures the amount of slack capacity available. Minimal market impact.

Initial Claims: Released at 8:30 A.M. Eastern time each Thursday. Report compiled by the Department of Labor. Initial jobless claims measure filings for state jobless benefits, which may give an indication for the economy regarding job growth or contraction. Minimal market impact.

International Trade, Import/Export: Released at 8:30 A.M. Eastern time around the 20th of each month. Report compiled by the Census Bureau and the Bureau of Economic Analysis, Department of Commerce. This report is important for insights into the overall trade balances, as well as trends in imports/exports of goods and services. The monthly trade balance can also influence the GDP forecasts. Typically has little market impact.

Leading Indicators: Released at 8:30 A.M. Eastern time in the first few days of the month. Compiled by the Conference Board. This report reflects previously announced economic indicators including new orders, jobless claims, money supply, average workweek, building permits, and stock prices. Very little market impact or interest.

National Association of Purchasing Management (NAPM): Released at 10:00 A.M. Eastern time on the first business day of the month for the prior month. This report, which is usually closely watched by the market, is a national survey of purchasing managers regarding new orders, production, employment, inventories, delivery times, prices, export/import orders, and related topics.

New Home Sales: Released at 10:00 A.M. Eastern time around the last business day of the month. Compiled by the Department of Commerce. Report reflects single-family homes sold and for sale. Minimal market impact.

Personal Income Consumption: Released at 8:30 A.M. Eastern time around the first business day of the month. Compiled by the Department of Commerce. Report measures income from all sources, including wages and salaries, and is used as indication for closely watched Employment Report. Also gives some indication of consumer demand. Some market interest and impact.

Philadelphia Fed Index: Released at 10:00 A.M. Eastern time on the third Thursday of the month. One of the widely watched regional manufacturing surveys, along with the Chicago Purchasing Managers index. Compiled by purchasing managers' organizations and Federal Reserve banks. Often viewed as an indicator for the National Association of Purchasing Management (NAPM) report.

Producer Price Index (PPI): Released at 8:30 A.M. Eastern time around the 11th of the month. Report compiled by Bureau of Labor Statistics, Department of Labor. PPI measures prices of goods at wholesale level, in the "crude," "intermediate," and "finished" categories. Finished goods index can be market-moving, as it reflects prices for goods that are ready to be sold to consumers.

Productivity and Costs: Released at 8:30 A.M. Eastern time around the 7th of the second month of each quarter. Compiled by the Bureau of Labor Statistics, Department of Labor. This measures productivity of workers and associated costs. The unit labor cost index can be market-moving during times of inflation, but otherwise this report seldom has market impact.

Retail Sales: Released at 8:30 A.M. Eastern time around the 13th of the month. Compiled by the Department of Commerce. This report measures total receipts of retail stores, the results of which are widely followed as an indicator of consumer spending. Some market impact.

Wholesale Trade: Released at 10:00 A.M. Eastern time around the fifth business day of the month. Compiled by Census Bureau, Department of Commerce. Report includes wholesale sales and inventory, but does not include personal consumption. Has little or no market impact.

Glossary

Advance-decline index: The ratio of advancing stocks to declining stocks. Over time, this index gives an indication of where the broad market has been going, a trend that is sometimes masked by indexes such as the Dow Jones Industrial Average, which contains just 30 stocks.

Arbitrage: The simultaneous purchase and sale of identical or equivalent financial instruments or commodity futures in order to benefit from a discrepancy in their price relationship.

Ask: Also called "offer." This indicates a willingness to sell a futures contract at a given price.

Back months: The futures or options on futures months being traded that are the furthest from expiration. Also called deferred or distant months.

Bar chart: A graph of prices, volume, and open interest for a specified time period used by the chartist to forecast market trends. A daily bar chart plots each trading session's high, low, and settlement prices.

Basis: The local cash market price minus the price of the nearby futures contract.

Basis contract: A forward contact in which the cash price is based on the basis relating to a specific futures contract.

Bear: One who believes prices will move lower.

Bear market: A market in which prices are declining.

Bearish key reversal: A bar chart formation that occurs in an uptrending market when the day's high is higher, the low is lower, and the close is below the previous day's. Can signal an upcoming downtrend.

Bid: The price that market participants are willing to pay.

Blowoff volume: An extraordinarily high-volume trading session that occurs suddenly in an uptrend signaling the end of the trend.

Bollinger Band: A trading band plotted at standard deviation levels above and below a moving average. Because standard deviation measures volatility, the bands widen during volatile markets and contract during calmer periods. The assumption used with Bollinger Bands is that prices tend to stay within the upper and lower band. When a price breaks through a boundary, either above the upper line or below the lower line, it usually signals that the move is strong enough to continue further. When the bands get closer together, it is more likely that there will be a price breakout.

Breakaway gap: A gap in prices that signals the end of a price pattern and the beginning of an important market move.

Broker: A firm or person engaged in executing orders to buy and sell stocks as well as futures and options contracts for customers. A full-service broker offers market information and advice to assist customers in trading. A discount broker simply executes orders for customers.

Brokerage house: A firm that handles orders to buy and sell stocks as well as futures and options contracts for customers.

Bull: One who expects prices to rise.

Bull market: A market in which prices are rising.

Bullish key reversal: A bar chart formation that occurs in a downtrending market when the day's high is higher, the low is lower, and the close is above the previous day's. Can signal an upcoming uptrend.

Buy on opening: To buy at the beginning of a trading session at a price within the opening range.

Car: A term used loosely to describe contract quantities.

Carryover: Last year's ending stocks of a storable commodity.

Cash commodity: The actual physical commodity as distinguished from a futures contract.

Cash price: Current market price of the actual physical commodity. Also called "spot price."

Cash sales: The sale of commodities in local cash markets such as elevators, terminals, packing houses, and auction markets.

Cash settlement: Final disposition of open positions on the last trading day of a contract month. Occurs in markets where there is no actual delivery.

Chartist: One who engages in technical analysis.

Clearinghouse: An adjunct to the futures exchange, responsible for settling trading accounts, clearing trades, collecting and maintaining performance bond funds, regulating delivery, and reporting trading data.

Close: The period at the end of the trading session. Sometimes used to refer to the closing range.

Commission: For futures contracts, the one-time fee charged by a broker to cover the trades you make to open and close each position, payable when you exit the position. Also called roundturn.

Commitment: When a trader or institution assumes the obligation to accept or make delivery on a futures contract.

Commodity exchange: An organization that formulates rules and procedures for the trading of futures and options on futures contracts, provides physical facilities for trading and/or access to electronic trading technologies, and oversees trading practices.

Commodity Futures Trading Commission (CFTC): Government agency that regulates the U.S. commodity futures industry.

Contract: Unit of trading for a financial or commodity future. Also, actual bilateral agreement between the parties (buyer and seller) of a futures or options on futures transaction as defined by an exchange.

Contract month: The month in which futures contracts may be satisfied by making or accepting delivery. Also called the delivery month.

Day order: An order that will be filled during the day's trading session or canceled.

Day trader: A trader who establishes and liquidates positions within one trading day, ending the day with no established position in the market.

Deferred pricing agreement: A cash sale in which you deliver the commodity and agree with the buyer to price it at a later date.

Delivery: The tender and receipt of an actual commodity or financial instrument in settlement of a futures contract.

Demand: The quantity of a commodity that buyers are willing to purchase from the market at a given price.

Double top, bottom: A bar chart formation that signals a possible trend reversal. In a point-and-figure chart, double tops and bottoms are used for buy and sell signals.

Downtrend: A price trend characterized by a series of lower highs and lower lows.

Electronic trading: Trading via computer through an automated order-entry and matching system.

Ending stocks: The amount of a storable commodity remaining at the end of a year.

Exhaustion gap: A gap in prices near the top or bottom of a price move that signals an abrupt turn in the market.

Fast market: Term used to define unusually hectic market conditions.

Fill-or-kill (FOK) order: A limit order that must be filled immediately or canceled.

Floor broker: An exchange member who is paid a fee for executing orders for clearing members or their customers. A floor broker executing orders must be licensed by the CFTC.

Floor trader: An exchange member who generally trades only his or her own account or for an account controlled by him or her. Also referred to as a local.

Fundamental analysis: A study of supply and demand to help project future prices of commodities. In stocks, fundamental analysis includes the characteristics of a company, such as assets, earnings, and revenue stream.

Fundamentalist: One who engages in fundamental analysis.

Futures: A term used to designate all contracts covering the purchase and sale of financial instruments or physical commodities for future delivery on a commodity futures exchange.

Futures commission merchant (FCM): A firm or person engaged in soliciting or accepting and handling orders for the purchase or sale of futures contracts, subject to the rules of a futures exchange and who, in connection with solicitation or acceptance of orders, accepts any money or securities to margin any resulting trades or contracts. The FCM must be licensed by the CFTC.

Futures contract: A standardized agreement, traded on a futures exchange, to buy or sell a commodity at a specified price at a date in the future. Specifies the commodity, quality, quantity, delivery date, and delivery point or cash settlement.

Gap: A price area at which the market did not trade from one day to the next.

Gap theory: A type of technical analysis that studies price gaps.

Good-till-canceled (GTC) order: An order that remains in effect until it's canceled or filled, or until the contract expires.

Head and shoulders: A sideways price formation at the top or bottom of the market that indicates a major market reversal.

Hedge: The purchase or sale of a futures contract as a temporary substitute for a cash market transaction to be made at a later date. Usually it involves opposite positions in the cash market and futures market at the same time.

Hedger: A person or firm who uses the futures market to offset price risk when intending to sell or buy the actual commodity.

Hedging: The purchase or sale of a futures contract as a temporary substitute for a cash market transaction to be made at a later date.

Initial performance bond: The funds required when a futures position is opened. Previously referred to as initial margin.

Intercommodity spread: A spread trade involving the same month of different but related futures contracts.

Intermarket spread: A spread trade involving same or related commodities at different exchanges. Also called an interexchange spread.

Intramarket spread: A spread trade involving different contract months of the same commodity. Also called an interdelivery spread.

Introducing broker (IB): A firm or person engaged in soliciting or accepting and handling orders for the purchase or sale of futures contracts, subject to the rules of a futures exchange, but not in accepting any money or securities to margin any resulting trades or contracts. The IB is associated with a correspondent FCM and must be licensed by the CFTC.

Leverage: The use of a small amount of assets to control a greater amount of assets.

Limit order: An order that can be filled only at a specified price or better.

Liquidation: Any transaction that offsets or closes out a long or short futures or options on futures position.

Long: Describes one who has bought futures or a stock to establish a market position and who has not yet closed out this position through an offsetting procedure. The opposite of short.

Long hedge: The purchase of a futures contract in anticipation of an actual purchase in the cash market.

Lot: The term used to describe a designated number of contracts.

Margin performance bond: A sum, usually smaller than the initial performance bond, that must remain on deposit in the customer's account for any position. A drop in funds below this level requires a deposit back to initial performance bond levels. Previously referred to as maintenance margin.

Market-if-touched (MIT) order: A price order that becomes a market order when the market trades at a specified price at least once.

Market-on-close (MOC) order: A market order filled during the close of a trading session.

Market order: An order filled immediately at the best price available.

Maximum price fluctuation: The maximum amount the contract price can change up or down during one trading session, as stipulated by exchange rules.

Minimum price fluctuation: The smallest increment of price movement possible in trading a given contract, often referred to as a tick.

Moving averages: A type of technical analysis using the averages of settlement prices.

Moving averages chart: A chart recording moving averages.

Nasdaq composite index: An index of all Nasdaq stocks, often used as a barometer of performance of smaller companies, although the index also includes larger firms such as Microsoft.

Nasdaq 100: An index based on the 100 largest stocks traded on the Nasdaq.

National Futures Association (NFA): A self-regulatory organization for the commodity futures industry comprised of firms and individuals that conduct business with the public.

Nearby: The nearest active trading month of a futures or options on futures contract.

Not-held (NH): A discretionary note on an order telling the floor broker that he or she won't be held accountable if the trade is executed outside the requirements of the order. This gives the broker discretion on getting the order filled.

Offer: Indicates a willingness to sell a futures contract at a given price.

Offset: Selling if one has bought, or buying if one has sold, a futures or options on futures contract.

Offsetting hedge: For a short hedger, to buy back futures and sell a commodity. For a long hedger, to sell back futures and buy a commodity.

Open outcry: The method of trading publicly so that each trader has a fair chance to buy or sell.

Opening: The beginning of the trading session.

Opening range: The range of prices at which the first bids and orders were made or first transactions were completed. Must be initiated by at least one trade.

Option: The right, but not the obligation, to sell or buy the underlying security or futures contract at a specified price within a specified time.

Order-cancels-other (OCO): An order that includes two orders, one of which cancels the other when filled. Also referred to as one-cancels-other.

Out-trades: A situation that results when there is some confusion or error on a trade—for example, when both traders think they were buying.

Overbought/oversold: A technical opinion of a market that has risen or fallen too much in relation to underlying fundamental factors.

Performance bond: Funds that must be deposited by a customer with his or her broker, by a broker with a clearing member, or by a clearing member with the clearinghouse. The performance bond helps to ensure the financial integrity of brokers, clearing members, and the exchange as a whole. Previously referred to as margin.

Performance bond call: A demand for additional funds to bring the customer's account back up to the initial performance bond level whenever adverse price movement has caused the account to go below the maintenance. Previously referred to as margin call.

Point-and-figure chart: A graph of charts with Xs for price increases and Os for price decreases, used by the chartist for buy and sell signals.

Position: An interest in the market, either long or short, in the form of open contracts.

Position trader: A trader who takes a position in the market and might hold that position over a long period of time.

Price order: An order to sell or buy at a certain price or better.

Pure hedger: A person who places a hedge to lock in a price for a commodity, and then offsets that hedge and transacts in the cash market simultaneously.

Rally: An upward movement of prices following a decline.

Range: The high and low prices or high and low bids/offers recorded during a specified time.

Relative Strength Index (RSI): A technical indicator developed by Welles Wilder to help investors gauge the current strength of a stock's price relative to its past performance. The usefulness of this indicator is based on the premise that the RSI will usually top out or bottom out before the actual market top or bottom, giving a signal that a reversal or at least a significant reaction in stock price is imminent. RSI readings above 70 indicate the shares are overbought and are likely to start falling. Readings below 30 indicate the shares are oversold and a rally can be expected. The time period specified determines the volatility of the RSI, with the shorter the time period the more volatile the reading.

Resistance line: A price level above which prices tend not to rise due to selling pressure.

Retracement: A price move in the opposite direction of a recent trend.

Runaway gap: A gap in prices after a trend has begun that signals the halfway point of a market move.

S&P 500: A widely followed benchmark of stock performance that includes 400 industrial firms, 40 financial stocks, 40 utilities, and 20 transportation stocks. All the firms in the index are large.

Scalp: To trade for small gains. Scalping normally involves establishing and liquidating a position quickly, usually within the same day, hour, or even just a few minutes.

Selective hedger: A person who hedges only when he or she believes that prices are likely to move against him or her.

Settlement price: A figure determined by the closing range that is used to calculate gains and losses in futures market accounts, performance bond calls, and invoice prices for deliveries.

Short: Describes one who has sold a futures contract or a stock to establish a market position and who has not yet closed out this position through an offsetting procedure. The opposite of long.

Short hedge: The sale of a futures contract in anticipation of a later cash market sale.

Sideways trend: Seen in a bar chart when prices tend not to go above or below a certain range of levels.

Speculator: One who attempts to anticipate price changes and, through buying or selling futures or stocks, aims to make profits.

Spread: The price difference between two contracts.

Spread order: An order that indicates the simultaneous purchase and sale of futures contracts.

Spread trade: The simultaneous purchase and sale of futures contracts for the same commodity or instrument for delivery in different months or in different but related markets.

Stochastic oscillator: A technical indicator developed by George Lane that compares a security's closing price with its price range for a given time period. The premise behind the stochastic oscillator is that when a stock is rising it tends to close near the high of the time period, and a falling stock closes near its low. Stochastics are plotted on a chart with values ranging from 0 to 100 for a specified time frame. As with moving averages, the sensitivity increases with shorter time spans. In general, readings above 80 are strong and indicate that the price is closing near its high. Readings below 20 are strong and indicate that the price is closing near its low. It is possible to modify the stochastic oscillator calculation to invoke a slow stochastic, thereby smoothing out some of the volatility in the indicator. Many technicians believe that the slow stochastic provides more accurate signals and is easier to interpret.

Stop close only order: A stop order that is executed only during the closing range of the trading session.

Stop limit order: An order that becomes a limit order only when the market trades at a specified price.

Stop with a price limit: A stop order with a specified worst price at which the order can be filled.

Symmetrical triangles: A price formation that can signal either a reversal or a continuation of price movement.

Target price: An expected selling or buying price. For long and short hedges with futures it is futures price plus expected basis.

Technical analysis: The study of historical price patterns to help forecast prices.

Tick: Refers to a change in price, either up or down.

Trend: The general direction of the market.

Uptrend: A price trend characterized by a series of higher highs and higher lows.

Volatility: An annualized measure of the fluctuations in the price of a futures contract. Historical volatility is the actual measure of futures price movement from the past. Implied volatility is a measure of what the market implies it is, as reflected in the option's price.

Volume: The number of transactions made during a specified period of time.

With discretion (DISC): A discretionary note on an order telling the floor broker to use his or her own discretion in filling the order.

(Glossary compiled from Chicago Mercantile Exchange online glossary at www.cme.com, MSN.com, and other sources.)

Useful Web Sites

AskResearch.com: Free charting service—however, using delayed data—for stocks and cash stock index markets, for both intraday and daily information. Useful for some preliminary research. (www. askresearch.com)

BollingerBands.com: Created by John Bollinger, best-known for his Bollinger Bands, this educational site offers a tutorial about Bollinger Bands, used as part of technical analysis. The tutorial includes how to calculate and use the bands. (www.bollingerbands.com)

Briefing.com: Free and subscription commentary on the stock market. (www.briefing.com)

CBOT.com: Chicago Board of Trade web site. Useful information on the markets and "knowledge center" for education and other resources. (www.cbot.com)

ClearStation.com: Offers education on technical analysis of stocks, including use of MACD (moving average convergence/divergence indicator). (www.clearstation.com)

CME.com: Chicago Mercantile Exchange web site. Useful information on the markets, as well as educational resources such as online courses on futures trading. Under "Prices," on the home page menu, the exchange also offers free interactive charts on end-of-the-day activity. (www.cme.com)

CNBC.com: This web site accompanies the television talk on CNBC. Videos of interviews and list of upcoming TV features also available. (www.cnbc.com)

CNNfn.com: The web site for CNNfn (the financial news broadcast of CNN). Company and market news featured. (www.cnnfn.com)

DTN.com: DTN (Data Transmission Network) provides real-time data and analysis, delivered to subscription customers by satellite and via the Internet, on the agricultural markets, financial services, weather, energy, and related markets and services. (www.dtn.com)

Lanston.com: Web site for Lanston Futures. Monthly and weekly calendar of economic events, as well as market commentary and Treasury updates available. (www.lanston.com)

NYSE.com: New York Stock Exchange web site, including "Getting Started" introduction to exchange and its workings. (www.nyse.com)

TeachTrade.com: "For traders, by traders." Founded by author Lewis J. Borsellino, TeachTrade.com provides dynamic market commentary on stock index futures as well as tools to aid in trading decisions. Market commentary reflects the same market research and technical analysis used by Lewis and his traders each day. (www.teachtrade.com)

TradingMarkets.com: Subscription site offering market commentary and online courses. (www.tradingmarkets.com)

Nasdaq.com: Nasdaq stock market web site, offering information on stocks, recent intial public offerings (IPOs), funds, and market indexes. Click on "Market Activity" for information on indexes. (www.nasdaq.com)

Yahoo.com: Finance section includes delayed stock quotes, free charts (on delayed data), as well as market updates and summaries and news digest for individual companies. (www.yahoo.com)

Index